RESPONSIVE HEARTS

FINE-TUNING OUR HEARTS TO GOD'S HEART

Truman Herring

& Tim Christian

Truman Herring Ministries

ISBN: 979-8-9850568-2-2

Photo 52945707 | Cardiogram Heart Hands © Syda
Productions | Dreamstime.com

Published by Truman Herring Ministries

The authors welcome your comments or questions.
Truman Herring: truherr@comcast.net
Tim Christian: tchristian@mabtsne.edu

Table of Contents

INTRODUCTION   5

1 – CHASTENING: WHAT IS IT? OUR PRIVATE DEVOTIONS   8

2 – CHASTENING: WHAT IS IT? GOD'S DISCIPLINARY ACTION   14

3 – CHASTENING DEVELOPS RESPONSIVE HEARTS   20

4 – THE FATHER'S LOOK   24

5 – THE FATHER'S REBUKE   36

6 – THE FATHER'S REBUKE NEEDED   40

7 – THE FATHER'S REBUKE: DELIVERED AND RECEIVED   49

8 – THE FATHER'S REBUKE A HOME AND CHURCH ACTIVITY   57

9 – A RESPONSIVE HEART IS MERCIFUL   63

10 – A FOOLISH HEART IS MERCILESS   69

11 – GOING HOME EARLY   85

12 – CHASTENING AND A SPIRITUAL AWAKENING   90

13 – THE FATHER'S FINAL CALL : A SURPRISING CANDIDATE   102

14 – OUR RESPONSE TO CHASTENING   109

15 – FORGET *OR* BE TRAINED   117

16 – DESPISE *OR* SUBMIT   121

17 – ROYAL SUBMISSION   130

18 – DISCOURAGED *OR* ENDURE   141

19 – STRENGTHEN YOURSELF IN THE LORD   148

APPENDIX

1 – DEVOTIONAL LIFE   155

2 – A DIFFERENT WORLD   157

3 – CHASTENING AND PSALMS 23, 32 & 51   162

INTRODUCTION

We know good things happen to bad people because of common grace. God "makes His sun rise on the evil and on the good, and sends rain on the just and on the unjust" (Matt. 5:45). Unless the bad person is as evil as Hitler or Stalin, this fact does not bother us.

The other side of the coin, however, does give us some distress. Why do bad things happen to God's people? If He loves us, why do we have troubles and trials?

The Almighty God could easily protect us from problems. As Jeremiah declared, "*Oh, Lord GOD! You Yourself made the heavens and earth by Your great power and with Your outstretched arm. Nothing is too difficult for You!*" (Jer. 32:17 HCSB). Yet, God does not protect us from all troubles. He could but He doesn't, so there must be a reason.

One of the reasons is the subject of this book. God allows difficulties into our lives because of His . . .

Chastening. "*If you endure chastening, God deals with you as with sons*" (Heb. 12:7 NKJV).

Discipline. "*It is for discipline that you have to endure. God is treating you as sons*" (Heb. 12:7 ESV).

Child training/education. "*God is educating you; . . . He's treating you as dear children. The trouble you're in isn't punishment; it's training, the normal experience of children.*" (Heb. 12:7 MSG).

Chastening, discipline, child training and education are varied translations of a neglected Bible word. I am confident the neglect is a result of misunderstanding rather than rejection. The misunderstanding is evident. Some imagine chastening is bad, even though God says it is beneficial. Others suspect discipline is child-abuse when it is actually child training. Contrary to what many believe, chastening is not evidence of God's anger. It is an undeniable evidence of our Father's love.

Right now God is working in our lives to fine-tune our hearts to His heart. He tenderly develops responsive, sensitive hearts in His children. Through chastening, the Father pursues an intimate love-relationship with you and me. When we understand how and why our Father disciplines us, our perspective on life's trials is transformed. By faith, we see a bright future even in our dark days.

Heart Problems

Every problem in our life is first a heart problem. We may blame others, time, or chance for limiting our potential and hindering our dreams. Yet, no matter where we place the blame, neither the devil, nor people, nor circumstances are our greatest enemies. Our greatest enemy is our own heart. The greatest hindrance to fulfilling God's greater purpose in our lives is insensitive, unresponsive hearts.

Seeker of Responsive Hearts

God is seeking responsive hearts. "*For the eyes of the Lord run to and fro throughout the whole earth, to show Himself strong on behalf of those whose heart is loyal to Him*" (2 Chron. 16:9). He searches throughout the entire earth. He searches up and down the streets where you and I live. He searches for loyal, sensitive, responsive hearts. There may be fewer than we would like to imagine, but we can be sure the Father will find every single one. None will be over looked. When He finds any loyal heart, He has found a person through whom He can work.

Do you want God to work in your life? Do you long for Him to do something special through you? Are you dissatisfied with the mundane mediocrity of your Christian life? You need a loyal, sensitive heart. Respond to Him and you will discover a wonderful reality. You will "*find [Him] when you search for [Him] with all your heart*" (Jer. 29:13), and you will discover that the Father was seeking you all along.

A Responsive Heart

I was a young man when I first read about Hudson Taylor (1832-1905), founder of the China Inland Mission. His life story impacted me deeply.

Hudson Taylor's testimony helped me see that God is more interested in a man's heart than a man's talent. Taylor's story gave me hope that if my heart was right with God, He could and would use me as well.

When Hudson Taylor was a young man, he sensed God saying to him, "I am going to reach inland China. If you will walk with me, I will do it through you." Taylor's heart was sensitive. He responded to God. He willingly said, "Here am I, send me."

The Father saw the loyal heart He was seeking in Hudson Taylor, and He showed Himself strong through his life. Hudson Taylor spent fifty-one years in China. Through Taylor, God called 750 missionaries to inland China. All were financed by faith as Hudson Taylor and the missionaries prayed. No solicitation or collections were allowed. Thousands of Chinese churches were planted, tens of thousands of Chinese people received Jesus Christ, and 125 schools were founded. God impacted the nation of China through one man with a loyal heart.

Loyal, responsive hearts are the ones through whom God works. They are the people who experience His supernatural favor. They are the people through whom God does His mighty work. Do you want to be one of those people? How is your heart?

Do you need a new perspective on your problems? Do you want to recognize your heavenly Father's work in your life? The following chapters were written with you in mind. *You can develop a sensitive, responsive heart.*[1]

---

[1] There have been drastic attitude changes toward the subject of God's chastening; people's views have changed while God and His Word remain constant. Please see Appendix 2, "A Different World."

Chapter 1

CHASTENING: WHAT IS IT?

Our Private Devotions

*"For whom the Lord loves
He chastens" (Hebrews 12:6)*

The baby-grand piano in our church's sanctuary is tuned regularly. The pianist told me it is needed, even when it sounds fine to me. My untrained ears do not hear what he hears.

The first time I watched a piano tuner work was educational. He began by playing chords up and down the keyboard. It sounded great. I expected him to say, "That's perfect. This piano doesn't need tuning." Instead he said, "Yep. I hear the problem." He then turned on a perfect-pitch instrument and played individual keys. When he found an offending key, he tightened or loosened the corresponding string. He fine-tuned the piano to the perfect-pitch instrument, one string at a time.

The Father, likewise, fine-tunes our out-of-tune hearts to His perfect heart. Chastening is one of His tuning tools. The Bible says, *"Whom the Lord loves He chastens"* (Heb. 12:6).

We begin with a definition of chastening so we will know what we are talking about. Notice several facets of the definition.

Chastening is Child training

The translated word "chasten," means child training that gives guidance and instruction for responsible living. Of course, the value of the instruction depends on how you respond. If you make a positive response, the guidance and instruction develops your ability to make appropriate choices.[2]

Child training has nothing to do with chronological age and everything to do with spiritual maturity. It helps God's "child prepare for adulthood [because] . . . God's goal [for us] is . . . maturity."[3] You and I need child training at 70 as well as at 7.

Chastening is also discipline. Several Bible translations state, *"The Lord disciplines the one he loves"* (Heb. 12:6a ESV, HCSB, NIV). Discipline helps us *"run with endurance the race that is set before us"* (Heb. 12:1d). "A successful runner must exercise discipline and submit to training."[4]

When I was young, I misunderstood both my dad's discipline and God's discipline. I thought they were bad. I thought chastening was always painful punishment, but I was wrong. Since, I have learned that I "never [need to] fear the chastening hand of the Lord; it is controlled by a loving heart."[5] *"For whom the Lord loves He chastens"* (Heb. 12:6a).

Like the heavenly Father, my dad disciplined me because he loved me and he used different methods. He talked to me, taught me, mentored me, demonstrated by his example how I was to live, and when I needed it, he spanked me. I once asked my dad why he was so strict with me and would not allow me to do what other dads allowed their children to do. I have never forgotten his answer. "Son," he said, "because I have high hopes for you." Why does our heavenly Father chasten us when others seem to live their lives as they please? He loves us and has high hopes and great plans for each of us.

How does the Father train and discipline us? What does He do to fine-tune our hearts? He chastens us through our devotional lives and with His disciplinary actions.

[2]Fredrick William Danker, *A Greek-English Lexicon of the New Testament and other Early Christian Literature*, 3rd ed. (Chicago: The University of Chicago Press, 2000), s.v., "παιδεία and παιδεύω; *paideia* and *paideuō*."
[3]Warren W. Wiersbe, *The Essential Everyday Bible Commentary* (Nashville: Thomas Nelson Publishers, 1993), 1579.
[4]Ibid.
[5]Ibid.

Our Devotional Life Fine-Tunes our Hearts

The "devotional life" refers to our daily Bible reading and prayer time. We set aside a time each day to devote our full attention to learning from and listening to God. Some call it a quiet time. The name is not important; the daily practice is the important thing. How does one have a daily devotional?[6]

My devotional life began in earnest when I was a twenty-year-old student at Louisiana State University. Since then, my daily devotional has been the dominant influence on my life and ministry. It is the source of nearly all of my preaching and writing through forty-five plus years of pastoral ministry. If I had understood the life- transforming power of a focused time in the Word and prayer every day, I would have started sooner.

I received Jesus Christ when I was nine years old. Until I was a senior in high school, my faith grew gradually but steadily. Like all believers, the Holy Spirit indwelt me from the moment I trusted Jesus Christ (1 Cor. 3:16). My parents made certain that my life was seeded with God's Word. Our family attended church every Sunday morning, Sunday night, and Wednesday night. This impacted me because "*faith **comes** by hearing, and hearing by the Word of God*" (Rom. 10:17, emphasis mine). God spoke to me through our faithful pastor's messages and through Bible studies taught by my Sunday school teachers. My parents' discipline taught me to respect authority, so I took what I heard from my pastor and teachers seriously. Dad read a few verses from the Bible and prayed before supper every evening, and I read some of the Bible on my own from time to time. My mother's prayers were also a major influence on my life.

My spiritual growth declined my senior year of high school. I continued to conform to the "Christian standard" (church attendance, no drinking, smoking, cussing), but inwardly I grieved the Holy Spirit with my private sins. The writer who observed, "Adult children can appear obedient when they are tuning out instead of acting out,"[7] could have been describing me.

During this time period, I heard a memorable sermon that convicted me deeply. God spoke to me through His Word. I knew I should

---

[6]You will find helpful suggestions in Appendix 1.

[7]Rosaria Champagne Butterfield, *The Secret Thoughts of an Unlikely Convert: An English Professor's Journey into Christian Faith* (Pittsburgh, PA: Crown & Covenant Publications, 2012), 116.

confess and forsake my sin, but I was willful. I determined to tune out rather than act out. I ignored the Father's voice and grieved the Holy Spirit. Even though He convicted me through several messages, I continued to resist. Consequently, my heart became more insensitive to God's voice and my spiritual growth stalled. I lost my passion to have a daily personal walk with God.

It was not the Father's rod, however, that turned my heart back to Him. It was the Father's gentle rebuke through a brand new Study Bible. Connie and I had been married for less than a year when I began to experience a great revival in my heart. My mother was burdened for our spiritual growth and gave Connie and me a new Study Bible. My mother prayed that I would have a new hunger in my heart to read and study that Bible. My mother's prayers were answered immediately.

God's Word and Our Spiritual Growth

The Study Bible seemed to attract my attention magnetically. Soon it became my constant companion. I carried it to college every day and spent most of my breaks reading and marking verses that spoke to me.

As I read God's Word, God's Word read me. I was convicted of my behavior over the past two years; I realized my heart had become insensitive to God.

A pattern developed in my daily devotional life. As I read and meditated on the Word, God called specific sins to mind. I was convicted of things that had not bothered me before. The Grand Piano Tuner was tightening the strings of my heart. Where I had become dull of hearing, I began to hear the Father's heart again. First John 1:9, *"If we confess our sins, He is faithful and just to forgive us **our** sins and to cleanse us from all unrighteousness"* (emphasis mine), became a precious and often used promise. New joy flooded my heart each time I was forgiven.

My time alone in God's Word created sweet fellowship, but it also made me aware of God's holiness. As never before, I realized *"God is light and in Him is no darkness at all"* (1 John 1:5). Again and again, God's light penetrated the darkness in my sinful heart.

One evening, when I was a boy, my friends and I gathered wood and built a campfire. We played around the fire, roasted hotdogs and marshmallows, and had a great time.

When I went home, I made a surprising discovery. Outside, in the dark, I looked as clean as when I started. When I walked into the light, I realized my hands and face and clothes were covered with sweat and dirt and soot. The light revealed what had been there, though unnoticed, all the time.

So it was in my relationship with God. As I read the Word, I walked in the light. The light revealed my sin. I confessed my sin and drew closer to God. The closer walk gave more light and also revealed more sin. The cycle of conviction, confession, forgiveness, cleansing, and fellowship was repeated again and again. But do not misunderstand. It was not a discouraging and defeating cycle. It was a victorious cycle. In fact, this is the normal experience of all Christians as we draw closer to God.

As I experienced revival, sometimes God directed me to apologize to a friend for my behavior during my backslidden days. One time I felt compelled to apologize for listening and laughing as others told dirty jokes. I tried to justify myself by telling God, "I didn't tell the jokes. I only listened. I'm not the guilty party." But the sweet fellowship with God was quenched until I obeyed. I confessed my sin to God, then went to my friend and apologized to him. He did not think it was a big deal, but my apology gave me the opportunity to share my salvation testimony with him for the first time. After being obedient, my rich fellowship with God was restored.

Another day as I was having my devotion time in the Bible, God reminded me of the day I picked up a "Playboy" magazine from a friend's coffee table to look at the centerfold picture. I confessed my lust and God forgave me, but I knew I had another responsibility. I had sinned against my friend as well as against God. I had to apologize for my unchristian example. My friend, of course, thought nothing of it. After all, it was his magazine. I did not judge my friend, but explained why it was sinful for me. I shared my testimony and told my friend how he could receive Jesus. Again, joy flooded my soul. We were friends, but I had never told him about Jesus. God used my witness, and a few weeks later, my friend trusted Jesus Christ as his Savior.

During this period of personal revival, God led me to make things right with several people. One of them was my former pastor. He welcomed me, and his counsel gave me valuable insight into a true pastor's heart.

Finally, I was impressed to return a crescent wrench I had borrowed from a construction job, but had never returned. I had rationalized that since I was going to return it, I did not steal it. In the midst of my personal revival, I had to confess to God that I was a thief. God forgave me, but I knew I must return the wrench. Humbling myself to God required humbling myself to the people I had wronged. Returning the wrench was a benchmark in my Christian journey. As I left the company office that day, I was filled with the Holy Spirit and with great joy.

More than forty-five years have passed since that day, and my daily time in the Word continues to be the source of my walk with God. Through my devotional life, the heavenly Father continues to chasten me and conform me to His image. If I neglect my time with Him, my heart soon grows cold and my flesh grows stronger.

Every Christian has the privilege of spending time with God through Bible reading, meditation, and prayer. The Bible is God's inspired book. He directed the very words the human writers recorded (2 Tim. 3:16). Through the years God preserved and protected the Bible. Now He speaks to His children through the Bible. He teaches us truth and directs us to know and do His will. The Bible warns us of sin and builds our faith (Rom. 10:17). We can apply the truths that God teaches us; we can be obedient to the Spirit's promptings as we develop sensitive hearts to God. A daily devotional time is a vital part of our personal, spiritual growth. God fine-tunes our hearts to the standard of His Word. Without it we may sound pleasing to the ears of others, but not to God.

Chapter 2

CHASTENING: WHAT IS IT?

God's Disciplinary Action

"For the Lord disciplines the one he loves,
And chastises every son whom he receives"
(Hebrews 12:6 ESV).

God not only trains His children through their private devotions, He also trains them through His disciplinary actions. The Holy Spirit lives inside each person who trusts Jesus Christ as personal Savior (Rom. 8:9). When we are tempted to sin, the Holy Spirit warns us to turn away from the temptation. If we disobey in spite of the Spirit's warnings, He convicts us of sin; He troubles our conscience. His conviction is an invitation to confess our sin, be forgiven and cleansed (1 John 1:9).

The Holy Spirit's conviction is good. God does not want us to be miserable; He wants us to delight in His mercy. *"He who covers his sins will not prosper, but whoever confesses and forsakes **them** will have mercy"* (Prov. 28:13, emphasis mine).

Our Father is active in our training. He coordinates the circumstances in our lives (Rom. 8:28). Sometimes He gets our attention through difficulties that awaken us, and sometimes through delights that humble us. God's patience and goodness should lead us to repentance

(Rom. 2:4). He knows what we need and how to get our attention. He uses various disciplinary methods.

Chastening Is Not Punishment

God's chastening is not punishment for bad behavior. Why?

Jesus Endured Our Punishment

Jesus Christ endured the punishment for all of our sins on the cross. God in human flesh (John 1:1, 14) fully paid sin's penalty (1 Tim. 2:5-6). Just before Jesus died, He called out, "*It is finished*!" (John 19:30), which means, "paid in full."[8] Jesus did not say, "I'm finished. I can't take any more. I'm dying." He cried out, "It is finished! I have paid sin's penalty in full."

Jesus Forgives All Sins

Jesus' blood cleanses all who receive Him through faith. His blood cleanses us from all unrighteousness, all sin, and all iniquity. His blood delivers us from all the punishment for all of our sins—past, present, and future.

"Then He adds, *'Their sins and their lawless deeds I will remember no more.'* Now where there is remission [forgiveness] of these, *there is* no longer an offering for sin" (Heb. 10:17-18). In other words, Jesus Christ's sacrifice is sufficient. No other offering is needed. Nothing else needs to be done to forgive our sins. We simply accept what Jesus has already done for us.

God's punishment results in permanent, eternal separation from Him. If we were punished for even one sin, we would spend eternity in hell.

Chastening, therefore, is not punishment for sin. It gets our attention. It corrects us when we are on the wrong path and directs us onto the right path. Chastening trains us for future obedience and blessings.

---

[8]John MacArthur, ed., *The MacArthur Study Bible* (Nashville: Word Publishing, 1997), 1625; n. John 19:30.

Chastening is God's means of restoring our fellowship with Him; it is His means of renewing responsive hearts within us.

Chastening is Good

The Greek word that is translated "chastening" (Heb. 12:5), appears in other New Testament verses. The various translations are instructive.

Chastening is *tender training*. The word is translated "nurture" in Ephesians 6:4. Paul exhorted parents to bring up their children *"in the nurture and admonition of the Lord."* The English Standard Version and the New American Standard Version translate the word, "discipline." The New International Version translates it, "training." We could correctly translate the verse, *"And you, fathers, do not provoke your children to wrath, but bring them up in the chastening and instruction of the Lord"* (Eph. 6:4, emphasis mine). Chastening is tender child training. Parents should avoid harsh, cruel discipline because it provokes anger. Children learn to obey through tender training.

Chastening includes *instruction*. Second Timothy 3:16 says, *"All scripture is given . . . for instruction* [chastening, discipline, training] *in righteousness"* (emphasis mine). Children learn through instruction.

Chastening can be *stern and painful*. Governor Pilate used the word at Jesus' trial. He said, *"I will therefore chastise Him and release Him"* (Luke 23:16, emphasis mine). Pilate tried to make a deal with the Jews. He offered to teach Jesus a lesson with a "whipping," but did not intend to inflict the much "more severe 'scourging' that [ultimately] preceded [Jesus'] crucifixion."[9]

At this point, we must avoid a serious misunderstanding. Two different Greek words are translated "chastise" and "scourge." Pilate offered to chastise Jesus—teach Him a lesson with a whipping[10] (Luke 23:16, 22). The Jewish protesters demanded His crucifixion, so Pilate tried to appease them with the far more severe scourging[11] (Matt. 27:26).

Sometimes the Father's discipline is painful, but it is never abusive. When God sends us into the furnace of testing, He always keeps His hand on the thermostat. He never places more on us than we can bear

---

[9]Robert H. Stein, *Luke* in *The New American Commentary*, vol. 24 (Nashville: Broadman & Holman Publishers, 1993), 580.

[10]*paideusas*

[11]*phragellosas*

(1 Cor. 10:13). Our heavenly Father does not scourge us.[12] No sane parent would be guilty of such criminal child-abuse. Sometimes a child learns only after a parent gets his or her attention with stern discipline.

Putting the details together, "chastening" is variously translated nurture, discipline, train, instruct, and whip. In Hebrews 12, the word includes all of God's various methods of child training. They are all good for us because they are motivated by love and given in wisdom with the purpose of our maturity. They are instructive and allow us to share in His holiness and produce the peaceable fruit of righteousness to those who respond correctly to the Father's discipline (Heb. 12:10-11).

A Limited View

When I was a boy, I had a limited view of my dad's discipline. I thought only of spankings. Now I know better. Dad used multiple methods. Sometimes he gave a look that communicated volumes. Sometimes he said a few words that corrected and directed me. Sometimes he spanked me. They were all parts of his instruction and my child training.

Likewise, God's chastening includes multiple methods. The Father draws us close, guides us into His will, and moves us toward spiritual maturity.

Chastening is for God's Children

---

[12]Someone may protest, "Not so fast. What about Hebrews 12:6? It says God 'scourges every son.'" Perhaps it is unfortunate that the King James, New American Standard, and New King James Versions translate Hebrews 12:6, *"For whom the Lord loves He chastens, and scourges every son whom He receives."* The Greek word, translated "scourges," is *mastigoi* (Heb. 12:6), not *phragellosas* (Matt. 27:26). Even though a form of the word, *emastigōse* (John 19:1), is used to describe what Pilate did to Jesus, *mastigoi* can be translated "whip," and is equivalent to *paideuō*, child training [Danker, s.v., "μαστιγόω; *mastigóō*"]. Other translations of Hebrews 12:6 use the word, "chasten" or "chastises" (ESV, NIV-2011, NET, RSV) instead of "scourges," and better reflect the meaning. "God's chastisement of us includes not only His 'whipping' us, as it were, for specific transgressions (with remedial not retributive intent), but also the entire range of trials and tribulations which He providentially ordains and which work to mortify sin and nurture faith" [Spiros Zodhiates, *The Complete Word Study Dictionary: New Testament*, 3rd ed. (Chattanooga, TN: AMG Publishers, 1992), s.v., "μαστιγόω; *mastigóō*"].

All who receive Jesus Christ are God's children, and all qualify for chastening. This is good. *"Behold, happy is the man whom God corrects; therefore do not despise the chastening of the Almighty"* (Job 5:17, emphasis mine). Be glad that God chastens you. The Bible says, *"For the Lord disciplines the one he loves, and chastises every son whom he receives"* (Heb. 12:6, ESV).

All of His Children

God trains all of His children. No one is exempt; no one is neglected. *"If we endure chastening, God deals with us as with sons; for what son is there whom a father does not chasten?"* (Heb. 12:7).

If you are not chastened, it is a warning sign. The un-chastened are not God's children. *"But if we are without chastening, of which all have become partakers, then we are illegitimate and not sons"* (Heb. 12:8). A lack of chastening is an urgent warning: you need to receive Jesus Christ as your Savior.

Only His Children

God is a faithful Father. He chastens *all* of His children, but *only* His children. Dad never went to a neighbor's house to instruct their children. He never spanked any of my friends. He only disciplined my three sisters and me. The Bible notes that *"we have had human fathers who corrected us, and we paid them respect."* It adds the application, *"Shall we not much more readily be in subjection to the Father of spirits and live?"* (Heb. 12:9).

The devil's children habitually practice sinful lifestyles (John 8:44). God does not chasten them. He sends warnings and witnesses. He convicts *"the world of sin, and of righteousness, and of judgment"* (John 16:8). He commands them to trust Jesus, but he does not give them child training. If they continue to reject Him, they will face a day of reckoning. The Bible warns, *"It is a fearful thing to fall into the hands of the living God"* (Heb. 10:31).

Many profess to know Christ but do not know the Father's chastening. Millions of professing Christians seldom attend church, serve to build the church, witness to the lost, read their Bibles, or give tithes or offerings to support the church. They are comfortable with a religious lifestyle that does not include continual growth in grace. They falsely rely on a time when they prayed a "sinner's prayer" and were baptized. The fact that God does not discipline them is irrefutable evidence that they are illegitimate children of religion but not true children of God. God does not sit passively by when His born again children sin. He actively chastens his children, and they know it.

The lost experience the consequences of their sin. They reap what they sow. God is longsuffering with the lost, "*Not willing that any should perish*" (2 Peter 3:9). God's longsuffering must not be misinterpreted as His acceptance of sin. My dad did not let me get away with anything and always explained why he disciplined me. Our Heavenly Father does even more as He changes us into the image of Christ, developing responsive hearts in us. If we are not changed we are not saved. If we are not constantly changing into Christ's image, God is not chastening us.

In summary, chastening is tender child training, not harsh punishment. Jesus Christ has already endured all of the punishment for all of our sins. Chastening is good. All of God's children are chastened because He is a faithful Father. In fact, chastening is a sure sign that one is in God's family.

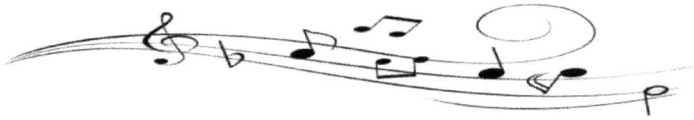

Chapter 3

CHASTENING DEVELOPS
RESPONSIVE HEARTS

In the early 1980s I pastored a church in Gresham, Oregon. One weekend our church had a retreat at a camp. Frankly, I was more excited about horseback riding than about anything else we planned that weekend. Even though I had only been on a horse once before, I thought I knew how to ride. I had seen lots of western movies and TV shows. What more did I need to know?

Morning Devotional

On the day of the horseback ride, God spoke to me through Psalm 32:8-9 in my morning devotional. The two verses use two illustrations. First, David describes tender chastening as instruction, teaching, and guidance. *"I will instruct you and teach you in the way you should go; I will guide you with my eye"* (v. 8). In contrast, he described stern chastening as a harness, bit and bridle. *"Do not be like the horse or like the mule, **which** have no understanding, which must be harnessed with bit and bridle, else they will not come near you"* (v. 9, emphasis mine). We can avoid the stern and respond to the tender.

Just as a parent's look can guide a child's behavior, God guides His children with His eye (v. 8). Obviously, we do not see a physical eye. God is invisible. Psalm 32:8 describe a spiritual reality. We see God's eyes and understand His heart as we read our Bibles. His Spirit reminds us of the things we learned at appropriate times throughout the day. This process is tender child training through a daily devotional.

Psalm 32:9 describe stern discipline. God's discipline is compared to controlling an impulsive horse or a stubborn mule with a harness, bit and bridle. If we do not respond to tender guidance, our Father uses stern discipline.

God wants to guide us by His Word. Our response determines the kind of chastening we receive.

Memorable Lesson

It so happened that my scheduled time for horseback riding was immediately after my morning devotional time. I went to the horse stables, excited about riding. A man led a horse to me and I stepped up into the saddle.

"This is a well-trained horse," he said. "Hold the reins while you ride, but don't use them to jerk his head. The bit will make his mouth hurt. Don't hurt my horse."

"When you are ready to go," he continued, "pick the reins up off of his neck and he will go forward. If you want to go left, lean your weight into the left stirrup. He will feel it and go left and if you want to go right lean into the right stirrup. Lay the reins on his neck when you want to stop."

I did as instructed and was amazed. The horse was sensitive to the gentle touch of the reins and to my slightest movements in the saddle. "Wow," I said, "this is easier than driving a car with an automatic transmission."

As I rode that well-trained horse, I continued meditating on Psalm 32:8-9. The heavenly Father seemed to say, "Son, I want you to respond to me like the horse is responding to you. I don't want to direct your life through pain. I don't want you to require my bit and bridle. I want you to respond to my tender look."

My horseback ride was a memorable object lesson. I wish I could say I have always been attentive to the Father's look, but I cannot. I have had a few jaw aches along the way. The taste of the bit and the pull of the reins were unpleasant, but they were good for me and led me back to the right path. I have learned that a responsive heart not only avoids pain, it also provides two additional benefits.

Holy Hearts

First, a responsive heart becomes a holy heart. *"For they [our human fathers] indeed for a few days chastened us as seemed best to them, but He [our Heavenly Father] for our profit, that we may be partakers of His holiness"* (Heb. 12:10, emphasis mine). The word "holiness" [13] translated is unique. It "denotes the holiness that is the essential attribute of God's character." [14] In other words, our human fathers try to change our behavior, but our heavenly Father can transform our character. Responding to His chastening reproduces Christ's character in us.

See the Father

Second, a responsive heart sees the Father. *"Pursue peace with all people, and holiness, without which no one will see the Lord"* (Heb. 12:14). The verse is not a warning to lost people. It is an exhortation to saved people. If we are unholy, our hearts will be insensitive; we will not see the Father's eye and will miss His tender guidance (Ps. 32:8). So, pursue peace and holiness. [15]

Profitable Pain

Chastening is not always pleasant at the time. Sometimes it is painful, but it is part of the Father's life-transforming process. It leads to fruitful spiritual growth. *"Now no chastening seems to be joyful for the present, but painful; nevertheless, afterward it yields the peaceable fruit of righteousness to those who have been trained by it"* (Heb. 12:11). When

---

[13]*hagiótētos*

[14]David L. Allen, *Hebrews* in *The New American Commentary*, vol. 35 (Nashville: Broadman & Holman Publishers, 2010), 582.

[15]"Beloved, now we are children of God; and it has not yet been revealed what we shall be, but we know that when He is revealed, we shall be like Him, for we shall see Him as He is" (1 Jn. 3:2). "Blessed *are* the pure in heart, for they shall see God" (Matt. 5:8).

I was a boy and my dad disciplined me, it did not make me happy but it was good for me in the long run. Likewise, God's chastening, while sometimes uncomfortable, is for our present and eternal good.

Four Levels of Chastening

God works in each of His children according to our individual needs. His child training is personal. If we do not respond to one kind of chastening, He uses another. His methods are many. He knows how to get results. I see at least four levels of the Father's chastening in the Bible. Remember, the goal of each level of chastening is to develop responsive hearts and draw us closer to His heart.

The first level of chastening is preferable: the **Father's look**. The second level is stern: the **Father's rebuke**. The third level is severe. If we ignore the Father's look and rebuke, we experience the **Father's rod**. The fourth level of chastening is irrevocable: the **Father's final call**. When all else fails, God takes His rebellious, unresponsive children home.

The following chapters explain and illustrate these four levels of chastening. Are you responding to the Father's chastening in your life?

Chapter 4

THE FATHER'S LOOK

*"I will instruct you and teach you
In the way you should go;
I will guide you with My eye"
(Ps. 32:8).*

When our sons, Jeremy and Matt, were eight and ten years old, both had a severe case of "WrestleMania." Wrestling was one of their favorite TV shows, and wrestling each other was their favorite activity. Hulk Hogan and other professional wrestlers were their heroes. They loved to wrestle and they loved to mimic the wrestlers.

Since I was the Commissioner of the Herring Wrestling Association, I made and enforced the in-house wrestling rules. The rules were simple; there were only three.

Rule 1: Do not wrestle in the living room.
Rule 2: You may wrestle in your bedroom.
Rule 3: DO NOT WRESTLE IN THE LIVING ROOM.

I explained the reasons for rules 1 and 3. "Boys, I want you to have fun, but I don't want you to be hurt. The coffee table in the living room has sharp edges. If you body-slam your brother in the living room, he might hit the coffee table and be seriously injured. One of you might end up in the hospital. Besides, Mom has lamps and other things in the living room that will break if you knock them over. Do not wrestle in the living room. Do you understand?"

"Yes, Daddy, we understand. We'll wrestle in our bedroom. We won't wrestle in the living room." They were sincere, almost angelic, when they answered. I was proud of them.

So, one day Jeremy and Matt were wrestling in the living room. I saw them and gave them "the father's look." No words were necessary. They instantly sensed my look and realized they were breaking rules 1 and 3. They stopped wrestling.

"Sorry Dad," they said. "We'll go to our bedroom." They did and I was pleased. They corrected their disobedience by responding to my look. My sons' response to me is a parable of our response to the Father's chastening.

An Example

Children do not respond to their parents automatically. They naturally rebel against authority, and parents are the first authority figures in their lives. That was true for every one of us. All of us are children of Adam. Though we are still in God's image, we were also born in Adam's image. We inherited his sin nature (Gen. 5:3; Rom. 5:19). However, parents can teach children; parents can mold their children's hearts.

David, the great king, Israel's deliverer, the man after God's heart, is a prime example. The Father's child training molded David's heart and prepared him for His greater purpose.

A Shepherd-Boy
Anointed as King

David entered the Bible's storyline, not as a heroic warrior, but as the youngest of eight sons. His dad, Jesse, assigned him shepherding duties. David was likely no more than 12 years old, but God saw his heart and was pleased. He was already passionately seeking God, maturing in his prayer life, and becoming a skilled musician and vocalist. David was young, but his heart was sensitive; he was learning to respond to the Holy Spirit.

King Saul was ruling Israel at the time. God saw Saul's rebellious heart and was displeased. He, therefore, said to the seer Samuel, "*Fill your horn with oil, and go; I am sending you to Jesse the Bethlehemite. For I have provided Myself a king among his sons*" (1 Sam. 16:1).

When Samuel arrived in Bethlehem, he asked to see Jesse's sons. As Jesse and his sons gathered, David was with the sheep. No one missed him. No one thought to call him. Everyone assumed the prophet's business was with the older boys. As each of Jesse's sons stood before Samuel, God said:

> *"Do not look at his appearance or his stature, because I have rejected him. Man does not see what the LORD sees, for man sees what is visible, but the LORD sees the heart." . . .*
> *After Jesse presented seven of his sons to him, Samuel told Jesse, "The LORD hasn't chosen any of these." Samuel asked him, "Are these all the sons you have?"*
> *"There is still the youngest," he answered, "but right now he's tending the sheep." Samuel told Jesse, "Send for him. We won't sit down to eat until he gets here"* (1 Sam. 16:7, 10-11, HCSB).

The family overlooked David, but God chose David. When David arrived, the LORD said to Samuel, *"'Anoint him, for he is the one.' So Samuel took the horn of oil and anointed him in the presence of his brothers."* When Samuel anointed David, *"the Spirit of the LORD took control of David from that day forward"* (vv. 12-13, HCSB).

God had been preparing David for his future calling. Neither he nor his family was aware, but God was watching his heart.[16] Obeying his dad was practical training. His years as a shepherd-boy were mostly routine and mundane, but no experience was wasted. Hours alone with the sheep became hours alone with God. Menial tasks were the Master's training. Sitting on a stone watching dad's sheep prepared him to sit on Israel's throne and protect the Father's sheep.

Our heavenly Father still uses common experiences to train His children. God is working in us, even when we are unaware. Do not despise your present assignment, no matter how menial it may seem. Jesus said, *"He who **is** faithful in **what is** least is faithful also in much; and he who is unjust in **what is** least is unjust also in much"* (Luke 16:10, emphasis mine). Small things, surrendered to the Father, make a big difference. You never know what God is preparing you to do.

Saul's Music Therapist

God used shepherding to further David's child training. He also used King Saul in the process.

---

[16]"Man sees what is visible, but the LORD sees the heart" (1 Sam. 16:7).

It was not long until others noticed David's spiritual gifts. The private preparation in David's heart made a public impact.

Because of Saul's rebellious heart, God removed the spiritual anointing to serve as Israel's king. *"The Spirit of the Lord departed from Saul, and a distressing spirit from the Lord troubled him"* (1 Sam. 16:14). One of his servants suggested a remedy. *"Let our master now command your servants . . . to seek out a man **who is** a skillful player on the harp. And it shall be that he will play it with his hand when the distressing spirit from God is upon you, and you shall be well"* (v. 16, emphasis mine). Saul thought it was worth a try.

Someone had heard David play and sing, and recommended him. David's music must have helped. From time to time Saul's aides summoned David to the royal court. Perhaps he played his harp behind a curtain, out of Saul's line of sight. Saul may not have seen more than a glimpse of David, if that much, during the music-therapy sessions. Further, Saul may have been unaware of people when the distressing spirit troubled him. Either one would explain why Saul did not seem to know David when he offered to fight Goliath (1 Sam. 17).

Notice God's progressive assignments. First, the unknown shepherd-boy sang praise psalms to God. His audience was a few sheep. Next, he praised God before his distressed, mentally deranged king. Later, he became famous as the *"sweet psalmist of Israel"* (2 Sam. 23:1). No matter the audience, David's focus was ultimately on His Lord.

In God's providence, David served when Saul was at his worst. He got a first-hand glimpse of a king without God's anointing. He observed, learned, and took the warning to heart. He did not want to be a King without God's anointing. He also became fast friends with Saul's son, Jonathan, during this time.

National Deliverer

David's child training prepared him for greater and greater service. He progressed from shepherd, to music therapist, to national deliverer. The occasion is one of the most famous stories in the Old Testament.

Saul and the Israeli army confronted the invading Philistine army a few miles southwest of Jerusalem. The two armies camped on opposite sides of the Valley of Elah.

The armies quickly fell into a routine. Each day, morning and evening, the armies formed battle lines. For several minutes, they shouted at one another and beat their swords and spears against their shields. Next, Goliath stepped forward from the Philistine line, cursed Israel in the names of the Philistine gods, and bellowed out a challenge: "Send your champion to fight me. If he kills me, we will be your servants. If I kill him, you will be our servants." The Israeli soldiers all ran and hid for a while, then both armies went back to their tents. This happened twice a day for forty days.

David's three oldest brothers were in Saul's army. Jesse sent David to deliver some supplies to his brothers and check on their welfare. David was still a teenager, probably 17 or 18. When he arrived at the battlefield he was shocked to discover that no fighting was going on. Providentially, he found his brothers in the battle line at the time Goliath was spewing out his defiant curse.

You remember, of course, that Goliath was about 9 feet, 9 inches tall. His armor weighed 125 pounds and his huge spearhead weighed 15 pounds. Even so, David was shocked that no one accepted the challenge. He heard Goliath's curse for what it was—an insult to God. David asked the Israeli soldiers cowering nearby, "*Who is this uncircumcised Philistine, that he should defy the armies of the living God?*" (1 Sam. 17:26). If no one dared to stand for God, David would.

David accepted the challenge on behalf of Israel's army. He went out to meet Goliath, armed with faith, his sling, and five smooth stones. Goliath was insulted to see a boy coming down to meet him. He roared, "*'Am I a dog, that you come to me with sticks?' And the Philistine cursed David by his gods*" (1 Sam. 17:43 ESV). David had correctly assessed the spiritual defiance in Goliath's challenge. Goliath sneered, "*Come to me, and I will give your flesh to the birds of the air and to the beasts of the field*" (v. 44 ESV).

David was un-intimidated. He said:

> [45] "*You come against me with a dagger, spear, and sword, but I come against you in the name of Yahweh of Hosts, the God of Israel's armies—you have defied Him. [46]Today, the LORD will hand you over to me. Today, I'll strike you down, cut your head off, and give the corpses of the Philistine camp to the birds of the sky and the creatures of the earth. Then all the world will know that Israel has a God, [47] and this whole assembly will know that it is not by sword or by spear that the LORD saves, for the battle is the LORD's. He will hand you over to us*" (vv. 45-47 HCSB).

You know the story. All the Israeli soldiers thought Goliath was too big to hit. David thought he was too big to miss, and he was right. With God's power, and hours and hours of solitary practice, David knocked the giant unconscious as one smooth stone zipped from his sling. The stone sunk into Goliath's forehead; his colossal, comatose hulk clanked face first into the grassy valley soil. "*David ran and stood over him. He grabbed the Philistine's sword, pulled it from its sheath, and used it to kill him. Then he cut off his head. When the Philistines saw that their hero was dead, they ran*" (v. 51, HCSB). David saved the day for Israel and became an instant national hero.

Notice the contrast. Without the Holy Spirit's anointing, King Saul, who was the biggest man in Israel's army, trembled at Goliath's challenge. With the Spirit's anointing, young David was courageous. He knew there was a cause, the cause was worth a fight (1 Sam. 17:29), and he acted, trusting God with the outcome.

David's private shepherding of his dad's sheep prepared him to publicly deliver the heavenly Father's sheep. David was trusted with great things because he had been faithful with small things (Luke 16:10). How about you?

David's Eyes Were On The Father's Eyes

I believe God wants us to live on the level of the Father's look. He wants us to respond consciously, consistently, and continually to His Word. He wants our daily devotional lives to make us increasingly sensitive to the Holy Spirit. Our private intimacy *with* Him equips us to perform public service *for* Him.

Saul and David are glaring contrasts. Saul cowered in fear; David was courageous by faith. Saul protected himself; David sacrificed himself. Jesus said, "*A hired hand . . . leaves the sheep and flees, and the wolf snatches them and scatters them. He flees because he is a hired hand and cares nothing for the sheep*" (John 10:12-13). Saul reacted like a hired hand; David responded like a shepherd. David not only delivered Israel, he was a type of Christ. He was willing to give his life for the Father's sheep (John 10:11).

God promoted David again. His influence and popularity blossomed, but his heart remained humble before God and man. David continued to serve Saul faithfully as a highly decorated army officer. He went "*wherever Saul sent him, **and** behaved wisely*" (1 Sam. 18:5, emphasis mine). The people celebrated David's victories. Women danced and sang, "*Saul has slain his thousands, and David his ten thousands*" (v. 7). Saul was insanely jealous and tried to kill David multiple times (1 Sam. 18-19). Finally, with Jonathan's help, David left the army and the royal court (1 Sam. 20).

Growing in Exile

David did not organize a *coup* against Saul. He chose to live in self-imposed exile in the Judean wilderness. Several hundred men joined him, but David waited on God.

God did not remove Saul from David's life. God used Saul to mature him. What Saul intended for evil, God used for David's good. It was all part of the Father's child training.

Likewise, God may use a Saul in your life. He may allow a painful person to distress you for a month, a year, or even longer. If so, it does not indicate a lack of love. God wants to use your trials to build your faith. The painful person is a part of your child training.

*****

Saul sent multiple search parties to find and kill David. Saul put him on Israel's "Most Wanted" list and declared him national enemy #1. Instead of going on the offensive, David did everything he could to avoid a confrontation. When a search party came near, David and his men hid. David did not return evil for evil. He was loyal to Saul.

One day someone saw David in the En Geri Wilderness and reported it to Saul. Realizing this was fresh, reliable intelligence, Saul took 3,000 soldiers to find and kill David (1 Sam. 24:1-2).

David was not surprised. He was aware of Saul's troop movements. He and his men were familiar with the terrain and knew all of the best hiding places. During a rest stop, King Saul went into a cave to take care of personal needs (1 Sam. 24:3). His security detail stood guard outside the cave. They did not realize David and several soldiers were inside with Saul.

One of David's warriors said, *"God has delivered your enemy into your hands. Kill him."*

The opportunity was a test of David's faith. Most of us would have agreed with David's friend. They were suffering under Saul's selfish reign. What could be wrong with eliminating the source of the problem with one slash from David's sword? Besides, God had rejected Saul and chosen David. Would not eliminating Saul be consistent with God's plan?

Chastening by Remembering the Word

David's men misinterpreted God's providence. Why? They were insensitive to the Father's eyes. Unlike David, they did not see the situation through the grid of God's Word.

How do you react to unfair treatment? Do you want vindication and revenge? Self-interest is natural, especially when well-meaning friends encourage an ego-enhancing response. The easy path, however, is often a detour from God's path.

How did David know God's direction in this situation? His heart was full of God's wisdom. The Pentateuch, the first five books of the Bible, was well known. David spent many hours in solitude, communing with God and meditating on His Word.

The Jewish people of David's era were not ignorant illiterates. They could read and write. The Psalms prove David's mastery of the skills; he was a gifted poet and wordsmith. Further, when he became King, one of his first responsibilities was to make a personal copy of the Pentateuch (Deut. 17:18).

David was well acquainted with Joseph's life in Genesis. He understood how God chose a young man and gave him a vision of someday delivering and leading his family. He knew that before Joseph became a leader, he was misunderstood, mistreated, and sold into slavery. In spite of his trials, God's eye was on Joseph. God protected and promoted Joseph after he patiently endured the Father's chastening. Joseph did not grow bitter toward God or his brothers. His eyes were on the Father's eyes. His heart was in tune with the Father's heart. When he had the opportunity to avenge himself upon his brothers, Joseph said:

> "Do not be afraid, for am I in the place of God? But as for you, you meant evil against me; but God meant it for good, in order to bring it about as it is this day, to save many people alive. Now therefore, do not be afraid; I will provide for you and your little ones." And he comforted them and spoke kindly to them (Gen. 50:19-21).

Joseph trusted the Father's heart when he did not understand His hand. Joseph's chastening (discipline, child training) prepared him for the Father's greater purpose—to save his family from famine. Even then, the Father's purpose was far greater than Joseph could see. Preserving Joseph's family was a stepping-stone toward transforming the family into a nation with a homeland.[17] The nation became the people *from whom*

---

[17]This fulfilled the land promise in God's covenant with Abraham (Gen. 12:1-3; 15:1-7, 13-14, 17-21).

Jesus was born. They lived in the land *where* Jesus was born. Do you see the amazing connection between Joseph's response to chastening and our redemption?

David knew God exalted Joseph in His time, in His way, for His purpose. He trusted God to do the same for him. Scripture was more than David's history book; it was the training manual for his heart. David's restraint in the cave and his running to attack Goliath (1 Sam. 17:48) were equally acts of courageous faith.

A Sensitive Heart

Stealthily, David slipped from the shadows, cut off the corner of Saul's robe (1 Sam. 24:4), and returned to hiding. Saul was oblivious. An exasperated soldier whispered, "If you won't kill him, I will," but David restrained his men.

"*Now it happened afterward that David's heart troubled him because he had cut Saul's robe*" (v. 5, emphasis mine). David had caught the eye of His Heavenly Father and his sensitive heart was troubled by his actions. At this level of child training, God conforms us into the image of His Son. Our actions and our attitudes are submitted to the Spirit's control. We are made partakers of His holiness. It may be rare for a Christian to daily and consistently live on this level of child training, but it is God's desire for each of us. We should long for such sweet fellowship with the Lord that anything that grieves His heart grieves ours. We are told to, "*Walk in the Spirit, and you shall not fulfill the lust of the flesh*" (Gal. 5:16). When was the last time that the Father's Look troubled your heart and changed your attitude and direction?

David cared more for the Father's look than for his soldiers' opinions. He said to his men, " '*The Lord forbid that I should do this thing to my master, the Lord's anointed, to stretch out my hand against him, seeing he is the anointed of the Lord.*' *So David restrained his servants with these words, and did not allow them to rise against Saul*" (vv. 6-7).

Saul finished his business and put on his three-cornered robe. He "*went on **his** way*" (1 Sam. 24:7b, emphasis mine) to continue his search for David. He did not realize the one he pursued had been his protector.

[8]After that, David got up, went out of the cave, and called to Saul, "My lord the king!" When Saul looked behind him, David bowed to the ground in homage.

Saul must have turned pale when he saw David at the mouth of the cave. Reality can be sobering.

⁹David said to Saul, "Why do you listen to the words of people who say, 'Look, David intends to harm you'? ¹⁰You can see with your own eyes that the Lord handed you over to me today in the cave. ⌊Someone⌋ advised ⌊me⌋ to kill you, but I took pity on you and said: I won't lift my hand against my lord, since he is the Lord's anointed. ¹¹See, my father! Look at the corner of your robe in my hand, for I cut it off, but I didn't kill you. Look and recognize that there is no evil or rebellion in me. I haven't sinned against you even though you are hunting me down to take my life.

Our hearts control our actions. Murder was in Saul's heart. Mercy was in David's heart. David continued:

¹²"May the Lord judge between you and me, and may the Lord take vengeance on you for me, but my hand will never be against you. ¹³As the old proverb says, 'Wickedness comes from wicked people.' My hand will never be against you. ¹⁴Who has the king of Israel come after? What are you chasing after? A dead dog? A flea? ¹⁵May the Lord be judge and decide between you and me. May He take notice and plead my case and deliver me from you."

¹⁶When David finished saying these things to him, Saul replied, "Is that your voice, David my son?" Then Saul wept aloud ¹⁷and said to David, "You are more righteous than I, for you have done what is good to me though I have done what is evil to you. ¹⁸You yourself have told me today what good you did for me: when the Lord handed me over to you, you didn't kill me. ¹⁹When a man finds his enemy, does he let him go unharmed? May the Lord repay you with good for what you've done for me today.

²⁰"Now I know for certain you will be king, and the kingdom of Israel will be established in your hand. ²¹Therefore swear to me by the Lord that you will not cut off my descendants or wipe out my name from my father's family." ²²So David swore to Saul. Then Saul went back home, and David and his men went up to the stronghold (1 Sam. 24:8-22 HCSB).

Do you think David was hypersensitive? His men certainly did. Because he was focused on the Father's heart, *"David's heart troubled him"* (v. 5). He was more concerned with the Father's look than his friend's criticism.

The old King James Version says David's "heart smote him." Does your heart ever "smite" you? Do your unkind words and actions "trouble" you? Have you grown comfortable with sin, or are you sensitive to the Father's look? Realize it or not, *"The eyes of the LORD are in every place, keeping watch on the evil and the good"* (Prov. 15:3).

God's Eye?

One may ask, *"How can a human see the invisible God? How does His eye guide us?"* (Ps. 32:8). Good questions.

God's "eye" is a figure of speech. *"God is Spirit"* (John 4:24), not flesh and blood. He does not have a physical eye, but He sees us inside and out. The Bible applies several human characteristics to God to help us understand how intimately and personally He relates to us. The terms are used to assist our limited understanding.[18]

Solomon appealed to his son. The exhortation explains how we can see God's invisible eye. *"My son, give me your heart,"* he said, *"and let your eyes observe my ways"* (Prov. 23:26). How could Solomon's son respond to his dad's heart and ways? The answer: *"My son, do not forget my law, but let your heart keep my commands"* (Prov. 3:1).

A son gives his heart to his father by trusting and obeying his dad's commands. As it is with a father and son, so it is with God and us. We see God's ways as we read God's Word. We listen and obey. We become *"doers of the Word, and not hearers only"* (James 1:22). In the process, our hearts are tuned to God's heart. We walk close to Jesus; His Word abides in us, and we abide in Him (John 15:7). Through hearing and doing, abiding and obeying, we become sensitive and responsive to the Father's look.

The Father's look is a spiritual reality and a practical truth, even if it defies physical explanation. How did my boys know I was looking at them when they were wrestling in the living room? I am not sure. They just knew. Parents and children have a connection.

My friend was a pastor's son. One day, when he was ten years old, he and a friend were sitting on the back pew, playing tic-tac-toe while his dad was preaching. He was whispering and playing and engrossed in his game when he felt something warm on the top of his head. He knew immediately what it was. He looked up, and as expected, his mother was glaring at him from the choir loft. She communicated with him from 75 feet away. How? I do not know, but she did. Parents and children have a connection.

---

[18]Theologians call terms such as God's eye, hand, arm, "anthropomorphic expressions."

How will you know the Father is looking at you? I am not sure, but you will. That has been my experience. Parents and children have a connection.

The Father's look is the first level of chastening. Are you in tune with Him?

36

Chapter 5

THE FATHER'S REBUKE

"My son, do not despise the chastening of the Lord,
Nor be discouraged when you are rebuked by Him"
(Hebrews 12:5).

Connie and I tried to raise our children with love and age appropriate discipline. When they were preschoolers, we gave simple instructions. We told them *what* they could and could not do. As they grew, we added explanations. We told them *why* they were to obey.

My first response to a disobedient son or daughter was to look at my child—the father's look. I wanted him or her to see my eyes, remember my instructions, and correct the behavior. As you might guess, my look was not always successful.

One day Matt and Jeremy were wrestling in the living room again. They knew the in-house wrestling rule: Do not wrestle in the living room. They knew why. The coffee table had sharp edges and the lamps were breakable. Yet, that day, they did not respond to my look. They paused momentarily, looked at me and at one another, and continued wrestling. It was time for the second level of chastening—the father's rebuke.

"Boys," I said, "I've told you why you can't wrestle in the living room. You know the rules." My stern tone got their attention. They heard and obeyed. "Sorry Dad," they said, and moved their match to their bedroom. Again, I was pleased.

Just as when I rebuked my sons, the Father's Rebuke is the second level of chastening. If we ignore His look, we hear his rebuke. The writer of Hebrews, quoting Proverbs 3:11-12, stated, *"My son, do not despise the chastening of the Lord, nor be discouraged when you are rebuked by Him; for whom the Lord loves He chastens, and scourges every son whom He receives"* (Heb. 12:5-6). "Rebuked" (v. 5) means to prove one is in the wrong, to reprove, to correct and admonish with child training.[19] Notice that being rebuked is a sign of our Father's love (v. 6). He does not say, "You sinned, so I'm washing my hands of you. I give up on you." No. He corrects us because He wants to restore our fellowship with Him.

Our Choice

The Father's rebuke offers a choice. We can receive it or ignore it. We can love it or hate it. According to Solomon, our choice is not an I.Q. (Intelligence Quotient) test; it is an M.Q. (Moral Quotient) test. Solomon said, *"Whoever loves instruction loves knowledge, but he who hates correction is stupid"* (Prov. 12:1, emphasis mine). That is why *"rebuke is more effective for a wise **man** than a hundred blows on a fool"* (Prov. 17:10, emphasis mine). Notice that "stupid" and "fool" are not assessments of mental capacity but of moral character. A "stupid" person is "a brutish person"; the word describes "one who stubbornly refuses to accept God's grace."[20] Likewise,

> Fool . . . is most often an ethical concept and goes beyond a lack of native intelligence. Although the fool might be one who acts boorishly, naively, or imprudently (e.g., Prov. 10:23; 20:3; cf. 21:20), he is more particularly one who lacks the wisdom which comes with the knowledge of God, someone who in his pride is wise in his own eyes but acts contrary to the will of God and thus does (intentionally or not) what is evil.[21]

In summary, a "stupid" person rejects God's grace and a "fool" rejects His wisdom. In both cases, pride is the problem. Rather than being

---

[19]Spiros Zodhiates, *The Complete Word Study Dictionary: New Testament*, 3rd ed. (Chattanooga, TN: AMG Publishers, 1992), s.v., ἐλέγχω, elégchō.

[20]J. N. Oswalt, in *Theological Wordbook of the Old Testament*, R. L. Harris, G. L. Archer, Jr., and B. K. Waltke, eds. (Chicago: Moody Press, 1999), s.v., בַּעַר, ba'ar."

[21]A. C. Myers, *The Eerdmans Bible Dictionary* (Grand Rapids: Eerdmans, 1987), s.v., "fool."

spiritually stupid or foolish, we can love and listen to the Father's rebuke. We can humble ourselves, receive His grace, and live according to His wisdom.

A positive response to the heavenly Father's rebuke rewards us with three desirable benefits.

Our Benefits

First, *we enjoy our Father's fellowship.* He said, *"Turn at my rebuke; surely I will pour out my spirit on you; I will make my words known to you"* (Prov. 1:23). The Christian life is not about completing projects; it is about a growing, intimate relationship with a Person.

Second, *we understand our Father's instruction.* "*He who disdains instruction despises his own soul, but he who heeds rebuke gets understanding*" (Prov. 15:32). Rebels damage themselves and darken their understanding. Spiritual confusion usually results from rebellious hearts rather than ignorant minds. We lack obedience more often than we lack information. In contrast, spiritually responsive believers are enlightened— we receive insight for daily living. If you have groped through a spiritual fog, you know the value of spiritual clarity.

Third, when we respond to His rebuke, *we obey our Father's will.* Solomon said, "*He who keeps instruction **is in** the way of life, but he who refuses correction goes astray*" (Prov. 10:17, emphasis mine). We have a choice. We can go astray or we can go His way—"the way of life." Are you following "the way to a meaningful life"?[22]

Just as I was pleased when my boys responded to my rebuke, God is pleased when you and I respond to His rebuke. We can know God's smile on our lives. We can receive His benefits—fellowship, understanding, and obedience—because we have a personal relationship with Him. We understand God's will and He empowers us to do His will.

King David experienced the benefits of responding to the Father's rebuke. His Psalms overflow with the reality of his intimate relationship with God. Psalm 23 is a classic example.

David enjoyed *fellowship* with the Father. He confidently declared, "*The LORD is my shepherd*" (Ps. 23:1). Years of shepherding his dad's

---

[22]Sid S. Buzzell, "Proverbs" in *The Bible Knowledge Commentary: An Exposition of the Scriptures*, vol. 1, eds., John F. Walvoord and Roy B. Zuck (Wheaton: Victor Books, 1985), 927.

sheep infused this confession with satisfaction and delight, confidence and security.

David received *understanding* from the Father. His circumstances, therefore, did not dictate his outlook. The Lord was David's shepherd and he was satisfied and delighted. He said, *"I shall not want. He makes me to lie down in green pastures; He leads me beside the still waters. He restores my soul"* (vv. 1-3). David had various kinds of enemies throughout his life, but he was confident and secure. He confessed, *"Yea, though I walk through the valley of the shadow of death, I will fear no evil; for You are with me"* (v. 4, emphasis mine). Spiritual understanding enabled David to see beyond his circumstances to his Shepherd.

David was *obedient* to the Father. He followed God's leadership *"in the paths of righteousness"* (v. 3). He was on the path to a meaningful life.

David praised God for the benefits of responding to His look and rebuke. His heart was tuned to the Father's heart (1 Sam. 13:14)—most of the time. Of course, like everyone, David was imperfect. Sometimes he became insensitive and unresponsive.

A responsive heart is not automatic. If we do not maintain our hearts daily, insensitivity grows. It happened to David, and it can happen to you and me. David responded to the Father's look in 1 Samuel 24. A short time later, 1 Samuel 25, he did not. Another painful person tested David, and he failed the test. At that point, David heard the Father's rebuke (the second level of chastening) through a surprising source.

Chapter 6

THE FATHER'S REBUKE:
NEEDED

The people in our lives are vital in our child training. Some are encouragers. They inspire us and build our confidence. Others are mentors. They have been where we need to go, and we can learn from their experience. Mentors challenge us to move beyond the *status quo*; they invest in us and instruct us.

Some of the most useful people in our lives are painful people. Someone described them as "heavenly sandpaper." They smooth the rough edges off of our personalities. We learn positive life-lessons from their negative examples.

Painful people invade our lives at inopportune times. They have a creative variety of personality disorders. Some are obnoxious narcissists.[23] If a true narcissist is in a power position, he or she is often cruel, abusive, and self-serving.

---

[23] "Narcissistic Personality Disorder" (accessed 6 May 2014); available from http://www.mayoclinic.org/diseases-conditions/narcissistic-personality-disorder/basics/definition/con-20025568. "Narcissistic personality disorder is a mental disorder in which people have an inflated sense of their own importance and a deep need for admiration. Those with narcissistic personality disorder believe that they're superior to others and have little regard for other people's feelings. But behind this mask of ultra-confidence lies a fragile self-esteem, vulnerable to the slightest criticism."

"Narcissistic personality disorder is one of several types of personality disorders. Personality disorders are conditions in which people have traits that cause them to feel and behave in socially distressing ways, limiting their ability to function in relationships and in other areas of their life, such as work or school."

As uncomfortable as it may be, God may use a narcissist, or a person with some other personality disorder, in your chastening. A problem person may be a significant influence in training you for future service.

So it was with David. Saul was one such person in his life; Nabal was another. God allowed these abusive men to torment David. But why?

The Father was training David to be the Spirit-empowered King of Israel. David was to shepherd God's people. He was to treat his subjects with grace and lead them with wisdom.

Saul was a vivid example of ruling without the Holy Spirit. David saw him as a self-centered, demonically tormented king. David experienced the conditions in Saul's court, and he was warned. Later, when he confessed his sin with Bathsheba, he pleaded, *"Do not cast me away from Your presence, and do not take Your Holy Spirit from me"* (Ps. 51:11). David did not want to rule without God's anointing.

Nabal was a memorable example of a graceless, foolish, ingrate. Before ascending to Israel's throne, David needed the personal experience of dealing with such a man. He needed to know what it was like to have his character assassinated and his service go unappreciated. He needed to know what it was like to be under the thumb of one who abused power, so that he would avoid abusing his power. David was a far wiser king because of Saul and Nabal.

Painful People and You

How do you deal with painful people in your life? Do you see them as God's test rather than God's torment? Like David, you may pass the test with one person and fail with another.

David both succeeded and failed spectacularly. He was attentive to the Father eye when Saul entered the cave where he and his men were hiding (1 Sam. 24). He had mercy on Saul; He willingly forgave Saul's murderous intentions. In contrast, David ignored the Father's eye when Nabal scorned his service and belittled his character (1 Sam. 25). He went into a murderous rage. At that point, David needed the second level of chastening—the Father's rebuke. Notice the reasons.

Wilderness Exile

David left the Israeli army and the king's court following Saul's repeated attempts to murder him. Twice he tried to pin David to the wall with a javelin.[24] When he left, assisted by Saul's son Jonathan, King Saul was furious. Saul placed David at the top of Israel's Most Wanted List. Saul wanted him "dead or dead."

David lived in the Judean wilderness to avoid a confrontation with Saul's soldiers. His family joined him, along with some four hundred men who were seeking justice and protection.

> *[1]David therefore departed from there and escaped to the cave of Adullam. So when his brothers and all his father's house heard it, they went down there to him. [2]And everyone who was in distress, everyone who was in debt, and everyone who was discontented gathered to him. So he became captain over them. And there were about four hundred men with him* (1 Sam. 22:1-2).

Saul's army searched for David but could not find him. A growing group of refugees joined David. Our Lord can both connect and protect. God regularly delivered David and his followers from Saul. David was under God's providential care. [25] Providence simply means "that frequently mysterious, always interesting way in which Yahweh *provides* for His servants in their various needs."[26] By the way, child of God, you too are under God's providential care.

God used trials to train David to trust Him daily. That is His goal for us as well. Jesus taught us to pray, *"Give us this day our daily bread"* (Matt. 6:11). He also said, *"Don't worry, saying, 'What will we eat?' or 'What will we drink?' or 'What will we wear?' . . . your heavenly Father knows that you need them. . . . Therefore don't worry about tomorrow, because tomorrow will worry about itself. Each day has enough trouble of its own"* (Matt. 6:31-32, 34, HCSB).

---

[24]1 Samuel 18:10; 19:9

[25]M. H. Manser, *Dictionary of Bible Themes: The Accessible and Comprehensive Tool for Topical Studies* (London: Martin Manser, 2009), s.v., "Providence." "The Continuing and often unseen activity of God in sustaining his universe, providing for the needs of every creature, and preparing for the completion of his eternal purposes." Henry W. Holloman, *Kregel Dictionary of the Bible and Theology* (Grand Rapids: Kregel Publications, 2005), s.v., "Providence." "God's gracious care of and governance over creation, especially directed at His own glory (Rom 11:36; 1 Cor 10:31; Rev 4:11) and the care of His redeemed people (Dt 1:30-33; Neh 9:6; Pss 37:28; 84:11; 104:27-30; 145:14-16; Mt 5:45; 6:30-33; Ac 14:17; Rom 8:28)."

[26]Dale Ralph Davis, *1 Samuel: Looking on the Heart* (Ross-shire, Scotland: Christian Focus Publications, 1999), 257.

As Saul's search widened, David moved his people further and further into the Paran wilderness (1 Sam. 25:1). *"The Desert of Paran . . . was situated on the southern border of tribal territories allotted to Judah* (cf. Josh. 15:3) *and thus provided the most isolated location within David's homeland for hiding from Saul."*[27]

Israeli Shepherds with large flocks were in the wilderness. Philistine raiding parties periodically crossed the border into Israel to kill and steal. David made himself useful. He became a shepherd to the shepherds; his men protected them. They took nothing for themselves, but were a trusted security force.

Nabal and David

Nabal, one of David's distant relatives, lived in Maon, a town in the Paran Wilderness. Maon was in *"the deep south of Judah, roughly eight miles south of Hebron."*[28] Nabal was a descendant of Caleb (1 Sam. 25:3), and the Calebites founded David's hometown, Bethlehem (2 Chron. 2:50-51). They were an esteemed family in Judah, David's tribe.[29]

Nabal was rich. He had 3,000 sheep and 1,000 goats (1 Sam. 25:2). David and his men repeatedly protected Nabal's wealth. David was a wall against Israel's enemies. Nabal lost no animals to raiders or to David.

Sheep shearing time came. Like the grain and grape harvests, shearing time was festive (1 Sam. 25:8). Carmel, where Nabal sheared his sheep, was a mile north of Maon. David sent ten soldiers to ask Nabal for some supplies to care for his growing group of refugees. Gifts were commonly given at shearing time to honor service rendered, show respect, and express friendship. David had every right to expect that Nabal would gladly share his wealth. [30] Without David, he may not have had a flock to shear. Further, David expected assistance from a kinsman in his time of need.

[27]Robert D. Bergen, *1 and 2 Samuel* in *The New American Commentary*, vol. 7 (Nashville: Broadman & Holman Publishers, 1996), 243.

[28] Davis, *1 Samuel*, 255.

[29]Ibid., 245–246.

[30]Eugene H. Peterson, *First and Second Samuel* in *Westminster Bible Companion*, eds., Patrick D. Miller and David L. Bartlett (Louisville, KY: Westminster John Knox Press, 1999), 120-121.

44

David's Camp

[4]When David heard in the wilderness that Nabal was shearing his sheep, [5]David sent ten young men; and David said to the young men, "Go up to Carmel, go to Nabal, and greet him in my name. [6]And thus you shall say to him who lives in prosperity: 'Peace be to you, peace to your house, and peace to all that you have! [7]Now I have heard that you have shearers. Your shepherds were with us, and we did not hurt them, nor was there anything missing from them all the while they were in Carmel. [8]Ask your young men, and they will tell you. Therefore let my young men find favor in your eyes, for we come on a feast day. Please give whatever comes to your hand to your servants and to your son David'" (1 Sam. 25).

Nabal's Camp

[9]So when David's young men came, they spoke to Nabal according to all these words in the name of David, and waited.

Things did not go as expected. Nabal's response was arrogant, harsh, and ungrateful; it showed his name was fitting. The Hebrew word, *nābāl*, means "fool."[31] "Isaiah 32:6 shows that a *nābāl* does not merely lack manners—he is a spiritual, moral, and social disaster."[32]

[10]Then Nabal answered David's servants, and said, "Who is David, and who is the son of Jesse? [This was an insult. He obviously knew David because he knew he was Jesse's son. David was already the most famous member of their tribe.] *There are many servants nowadays who break away each one from his master.* [Was he siding with Saul? Perhaps. More likely, he was simply being obnoxious.] *[11]Shall I then take my* [Note the narcissism in the 7 personal pronouns: "I" and "my."] *bread and my water and my meat that I have killed for my shearers, and give it to men when I do not know where they are from?"*

---

[31]F. Brown, S. R. Driver, and C. A. Briggs, *Enhanced Brown-Driver-Briggs Hebrew and English Lexicon* (Oak Harbor, WA: Logos Research Systems, 2000), s.v., "נָבָל; *nābāl*." See Psalm 14:1.

[32]Davis, *1 Samuel*, 255-56. "For a fool speaks foolishness and his mind plots iniquity. He lives in a godless way and speaks falsely about the LORD. He leaves the hungry empty and deprives the thirsty of drink" (Isa. 32:6, HCSB).

David's Camp

[12]So David's young men turned on their heels and went back; and they came and told him all these words.

For David, Nabal's response was not an "I.Q." test; it was a "M.Q." (Moral Quotient) test. Would David be wise or foolish? Would he look to the Father or react in the flesh? Would the Father's eye guide him or would his anger control him?

When people offend, misrepresent, and mistreat you, you too face an M.Q. test. Will you react in anger or will you ask God what He wants you to do? Your response determines whether your trials will grow your faith and wisdom, or multiply your fears and doubts (James 1:5-6).[33]

David made a split-second decision. He decided to make a personal appearance at Nabal's camp, but it would not be a social visit. *"Then David said to his men, 'Every man gird on his sword.' So every man girded on his sword, and David also girded on his sword. And about four hundred men went with David, and two hundred stayed with the supplies"* (v. 13).[34]

The sword David refused to use on Saul (1 Sam. 24:4-6), he fully intended to use on Nabal. David looked horizontally at the circumstances and felt justified taking matters into his own hands. He reacted in the flesh instead of responding in the Spirit.

David ignored the first level of chastening. He was insensitive to the Father's look. Unless the Father got David's attention with the second level of chastening, blood (and a lot of it) was about to flow.

Nabal was ill mannered, ungrateful, and obnoxious. He tested David's faith and David failed the test. God's law did not give David the freedom to execute Nabal, much less the innocent people who were with him. To the contrary, God said, *"You shall not take vengeance, nor bear any grudge against the children of your people, but you shall love your neighbor as yourself: I am the Lord"* (Lev. 19:18). God promised to deal with problem people in His time and way. He said, *"Vengeance belongs to Me; I will repay. In time their foot will slip, for their day of disaster is near, and their doom is coming quickly"* (Deut. 32:35, HCSB).

---

[33]"If any of you lacks wisdom, let him ask of God, who gives to all liberally and without reproach, and it will be given to him. But let him ask in faith, with no doubting, for he who doubts is like a wave of the sea driven and tossed by the wind" (James 1:5-6).

[34]Notice, the ranks of his refugees had swelled by another two hundred.

Misapplying Scripture

If we ignore the Scriptures, our hearts become insensitive. Instead of applying Scripture to our situation, we may twist and misapply Bible verses to justify ourselves.

When a friend was a young, naïve pastor, a man went to him for pastoral counseling. The man's heart was broken. He had recently discovered his wife's unfaithfulness. With great piety and concern for her spiritual condition he asked, "Can God forgive her?"

My friend misunderstood. He thought the husband's question was sincere. He did not realize the man was asking, "Pastor, can you see how I've been mistreated? Have you ever heard of anything so unfair? I'm hurt. I'm innocent. She's guilty, guilty, guilty. Could you call her and condemn her for me? Can you make her feel like the worm she is?"

The pastor assured the husband that God could and would forgive his wife. Again, that was what he thought the man wanted to know. My friend reminded him of David, Bathsheba, and Uriah. At the mention of Uriah's murder and God's forgiveness, the man's face brightened. With obvious excitement over a newly discovered truth he asked, "Does that mean I can kill both of them?" My friend was blind-sided by the question, but managed to discourage the proposed murders. However, you can see the problem. The wounded man was ready to twist the Scriptures to justify his desire for revenge.

And that was David's attitude as he headed for Nabal's camp. He declared a self-righteous and self-justifying oath. "*May God do so, and more also, to the enemies of David, if I leave one male of all who belong to him by morning light*" (1 Sam. 25:22). "David's oath . . . essentially obligated God to kill any enemies that David himself might fail to kill.[35] Contrary to the Scripture, "You shall not take vengeance," David determined to avenge himself. He convinced himself it was right, God was in agreement, and God was obligated to partner with him on his mission of personal revenge.

Two of Jesus' disciples portray a similar attitude. One day Jesus planned to go into a Samaritan city. He sent messengers to prepare for his visit, but the people in the city rejected them. They responded to Jesus' messengers much like Nabal responded to David's messengers. Notice the difference between what Jesus' disciples wanted to do and what Jesus chose to do.

---

[35]Bergen, 248.

> *[Jesus] sent messengers . . . And . . . they entered a village of the Samaritans, to prepare for Him. *[53]*But they did not receive Him . . . *[54]*And when His disciples James and John saw this, they said, "Lord, do You want us to command fire to come down from heaven and consume them, just as Elijah did?"*
>
> [55]*But He turned and rebuked them, and said, "You do not know what manner of spirit you are of. *[56]*For the Son of Man did not come to destroy men's lives but to save them." And they went to another village* (Luke 9:52-26).

David's heart was not in tune with the Father's heart—he did not have what we now call the mind of Christ (Phil. 2:5). Instead, David was like Jesus' vengeful disciples and like my friend's vengeful parishioner. David thought his wrath against Nabal was justified. David needed the Father's rebuke to protect him from himself.

Conclusion

Hindsight is 20/20. After the fact, it is easy to see what David should have done to maintain a responsive heart. He should have:

- Depended on God's providence in every situation.
- Trusted God to deal with Nabal, his painful person.
- Expected his faith to be tested.
- Obeyed God's Word rather than twisting and misapplying it.

He should have and could have, and his heart would have remained sensitive to the Father's eye. But he did not. Sound familiar?

Pause for a moment to consider your own heart. Does God need to protect you from yourself? Have you become insensitive to the Father's look? David and Nabal's story reminds us that without heart maintenance, insensitivity will grow. It can grow quickly, and the results may be disastrous.

David's need for the second level of chastening was obvious. "Should've" and "could've" do not change reality. Review David's symptoms.

- He ignored the Father's eye.

- He failed the M. Q. test. David reacted in anger instead of looking to the Father.
- He did not consider a painful person's usefulness in his life.
- His pride was offended.
- He demanded vindication. David did not trust God with the painful person.
- He planned violent personal revenge.
- He ignored and misapplied Scripture.
- He justified his anger and actions.

Do you recognize any of David's attitudes and actions in your heart? If so, expect the Father's rebuke.

Chapter 7

THE FATHER'S REBUKE:
DELIVERED AND RECEIVED

The story turned from David's anger, to his encounter with Nabal's wife. Abigail was God's messenger to David. She delivered the Father's rebuke.

What kind of person will deliver God's rebuke to you? God may speak through one in a position of authority, such as a pastor, teacher, or mentor. But it is just as likely He will speak to you through a peer. A friend or a spouse may deliver God's rebuke. Receiving and responding to the rebuke, no matter the source, requires humility.

Notice another side of the question. If you presently have a responsive heart, do you qualify to deliver God's rebuke to another believer? Abigail's character is instructive. The qualities in her life can be in you as well.

Nabal's House

The drama continued. Up to this point, the record ping-ponged our attention between David and Nabal. Now Abigail entered the picture, and she was a welcome sight.

Abigail was Nabal's greatest asset. Nabal married far above himself. Abigail was wise and winsome, gracious and gorgeous; she was Nabal's better half and polar opposite. Notice the contrast between the two. *"She was a woman of good understanding and beautiful appearance; but the man was harsh and evil in his doings"* (1 Sam. 25:3).

A young man heard Nabal insult David's men and sized up the situation. He knew David's abilities and anticipated his response. Wisely, he rushed to Abigail. The young man's report did not flatter Nabal, but it recognized the urgency of the moment.

> *[14]Now one of the young men told Abigail, Nabal's wife, saying, "Look, David sent messengers from the wilderness to greet our master; and he reviled them. [15]But the men were very good to us, and we were not hurt, nor did we miss anything as long as we accompanied them, when we were in the fields. [16]They were a wall to us both by night and day, all the time we were with them keeping the sheep. [17]Now therefore, know and consider what you will do, for harm is determined against our master and against all his household. For he is such a scoundrel that one cannot speak to him"* (1 Sam. 25).

Abigail knew her husband made a foolish response. She rushed to rectify the situation if she could.

> *[18]Then Abigail made haste and took two hundred loaves of bread, two skins of wine, five sheep already dressed, five seahs of roasted grain, one hundred clusters of raisins, and two hundred cakes of figs, and loaded them on donkeys. [19]And she said to her servants, "Go on before me; see, I am coming after you." But she did not tell her husband Nabal.*

The gift was sizable. It took two or more donkeys to carry it all. The amount of food, however, "would not have been enough to feed six hundred men plus their families for any length of time, but it did represent a sizable token of appreciation and support for a fellow Judahite."[36]

On the Road to Nabal's Camp

The narrative shifted again. David was talking to his men as they traveled toward Nabal's camp. He was justifying his anger and attack plan.

---

[36]Ibid.

He was preparing them to unleash his wrath upon Nabal when Abigail appeared.

> [20]*So it was, as she rode on the donkey, that she went down under cover of the hill; and there were David and his men, coming down toward her, and she met them.* [21]*Now David had said, "Surely in vain I have protected all that this fellow has in the wilderness, so that nothing was missed of all that belongs to him. And he has repaid me evil for good.* [22]*May God do so, and more also, to the enemies of David, if I leave one male of all who belong to him by morning light"*
> (1 Sam. 25).

Make the Best of a Bad Situation

And so we come to the first character quality that prepared Abigail to deliver God's message to David. She made the best of her bad situation. She refused to be a victim. Rather than moan about the unfairness of her problems, she did what she could to solve them.

Abigail's life was not easy. It is unlikely that Nabal was more considerate of her than of anyone else. But in spite of her imperfect life, she chose to make the best of a bad situation. She made a wise choice.

Some Christians waste their energy moaning and groaning about life's unfairness and inequities. They live in perpetual disappointment, blaming God, circumstances, and other people. They do not take personal responsibility for facing life's challenges. One author's insight is helpful. He wrote:

> Life is difficult.
> This is a great truth, . . . because once we truly see this truth, we transcend it. . . .
> Most do not fully see this truth that life is difficult. Instead they moan more or less incessantly, noisily or subtly, about the enormity of their problems, their burdens, and their difficulties as if life were generally easy, as if life *should* be easy. They voice their belief, noisily or subtly, that their difficulties represent a unique kind of affliction that should not be and that has somehow been especially visited upon them, or else upon their families, their tribe, their class, their nation, their race or even their species, and not upon others. I know about this moaning because I have done my share.

Life is a series of problems. Do we want to moan about them or solve them? Do we want to teach our children to solve them?[37]

Abigail chose to solve problems rather than moan about them, even when life was unfair. She chose not to expect perfection in this life.

We do not know if Abigail regretted her marriage to Nabal. Likely, she gave it little thought. Her father probably arranged the marriage and she did her duty. She married Nabal, and he became part of her child training. She did not despise chastening or become discouraged. She endured and submitted (Heb. 12:5, 7, 9) and, thereby, was spiritually prepared to fulfill God's greater purpose for her life. She did not yet see that purpose; she was simply doing all she could to make the best of a bad situation.

Many would improve their attitude by adopting Abigail's approach to life's realities. How about you? Are you making the best of your hardships?

Abigail Spoke to David

Abigail approached David with respect. She did not know how he would respond.

[23]Now when Abigail saw David, she dismounted quickly from the donkey, fell on her face before David, and bowed down to the ground. [24]So she fell at his feet and said: "On me, my lord, on me let this iniquity be! And please let your maidservant speak in your ears, and hear the words of your maidservant.

Abigail was acutely aware of her husband's deficiencies. She said, *"Please, let not my lord regard this scoundrel Nabal. For as his name is, so is he: Nabal is his name, and folly is with him! But I, your maidservant, did not see the young men of my lord whom you sent"* (v. 25).

Abigail's appeal to David revealed profound spiritual wisdom. She said, *"Now therefore, my lord, as the LORD lives and as your soul lives, since the LORD has held you back from coming to bloodshed and from avenging yourself with your own hand, now then, let your enemies and those who seek harm for my lord be as Nabal"* (v. 26). She gave God the credit for preventing David from avenging himself, but God was using

---

[37]M. Scott Peck, *The Road Less Traveled: A New Psychology of Love, Traditional Values and Spiritual Growth* (New York: Touchstone, 1978, 2003), 15. The quote is helpful in our context, but is not intended as an endorsement of the book, nor as a recommendation of Peck's other books.

her to pull back on the reins. God sent Abigail to stop David before he reached Nabal's camp.

Has someone told you an uncomfortable truth about yourself? Could it be that God is speaking to you through that person? Did you accept the rebuke or become angry with the messenger?

Abigail continued, "*And now this present which your maidservant has brought to my lord, let it be given to the young men who follow my lord*" (v. 27). She delivered the gift her husband should have given. It was intended to appease David's anger. It was also an appeal for reconciliation. She added, "*Please forgive the trespass of your maidservant*" (v. 28a). Though innocent, Abigail accepted the guilt of the blameworthy. Do you see anyone else's shadow in this picture?[38]

Abigail was blessed for humbly speaking the truth and taking decisive action. She was a peacemaker; she did the Father's work. The same will be true for us. Our Lord Jesus said, "*Blessed are the peacemakers, for they shall be called sons of God*" (Matt. 5:9). We too can be peacemakers. We can make the best of our bad situation.

Focus on God's Greater Purpose

Second, as Abigail did, we can focus on God's greater purpose. He is using our present circumstances to prepare us for greater usefulness in the future.

Abigail understood God's future plans for David and Israel. We do not know how she knew. Likely, the subject had been discussed among David's relatives in Maon. Perhaps they knew Samuel had anointed David to be the next king. Nabal certainly knew David had fled into the Paran Desert to escape from Saul (v. 10). At any rate, Abigail reminded David of his greater purpose.

> [28] . . . *for the LORD will certainly make for my lord an enduring house, because my lord fights the battles of the LORD, and evil is not found in you throughout your days.* [29]*Yet a man has risen to pursue you and seek your life, but the life of my lord shall be bound in the bundle of the living with the LORD your God; and the lives of your enemies He shall sling out, as from the pocket of a sling.*

---

[38]Jesus Christ "bore our sins in His own body on the tree" (1 Peter 2:24). "For Christ also suffered once for sins, the just for the unjust, that He might bring us to God" (1 Peter 3:18).

Notice Abigail's picturesque language. She reminded David that his security was in the Lord. His "life" was "bound in" the LORD's "bundle." Like a pouch of gold coins, bound into a man's travel bundle, David was God's precious property. He was secure. He belonged to God. He could trust God's protection. "David," she said, "God is holding you close. Trust Him with your enemies; they will be slung away, like a stone from a sling." God may have used this figure of speech as a subtle reminder of how God had protected David when he faced Goliath with nothing but his faith and his sling.

Abigail reminded David to fight the Lord's battles instead of his own. "God has a greater purpose for you, David. Petty vindictiveness is beneath a man with your future." She said:

> [30]*And it shall come to pass, when the LORD has done for my lord according to all the good that He has spoken concerning you, and has appointed you ruler over Israel,* [31]*that this will be no grief to you, nor offense of heart to my lord, either that you have shed blood without cause, or that my lord has avenged himself. But when the LORD has dealt well with my lord, then remember your maidservant."*

Abigail's speech is amazing. She noted that, up to this point, David was pure and was fulfilling God's greater purpose (v. 28b). She knew Saul's persecution of David was unjust, and assured David of God's protection (v. 29). Abigail reasoned that if God was going to fulfill His great promises to David, He would obviously deal with this minor situation (vv. 30-31). "To encourage David to choose the path of peace and forgiveness in this matter, Abigail brought before David a prophetic vision of his destiny. David should act magnanimously in the present situation because God has designed a majestic future for him."[39] She warned David that a petty act of revenge on this occasion could come back to haunt him in the future (v. 31).

David Spoke to Abigail

Fortunately David listened and learned. He received God's rebuke through Abigail.

---

[39]Bergen, 250.

³²Then David said to Abigail: "Blessed is the LORD God of Israel, who sent you this day to meet me! ³³And blessed is your advice and blessed are you, because you have kept me this day from coming to bloodshed and from avenging myself with my own hand. ³⁴For indeed, as the LORD God of Israel lives, who has kept me back from hurting you, unless you had hurried and come to meet me, surely by morning light no males would have been left to Nabal!" ³⁵So David received from her hand what she had brought him, and said to her, "Go up in peace to your house. See, I have heeded your voice and respected your person."

Abigail was the star of the story. Not only did she rescue her husband from David, she rescued David from himself. David followed Abigail's advice. He respected and submitted to the father's second level of chastening—His rebuke through Abigail. David wisely left Nabal in God's hands.

If we ignore the Father's eye, He is faithful to send a rebuke. It will require humility, but we can respond positively no matter whom God uses to deliver His rebuke.

Wait on God's Solutions

Third, like Abigail, we can wait on God's solutions. Isaiah's promise is applicable today. *"But those who wait on the Lord shall renew **their** strength; they shall mount up with wings like eagles, they shall run and not be weary, they shall walk and not faint"* (Isa. 40:31).

Abigail returned home to find a drunken party going on in her house. She waited until the next morning when her husband was sober, then told him about her gift to David. Apparently, he became so enraged that it induced a paralyzing stroke. *"He became like a stone"* and died ten days later (1 Sam. 25:36-38).

God did a surprising thing. His solution was far better than David's vindictive plan. God dealt with Nabal without any collateral damage.

It is still wise to wait on God's solutions. He can work things out in ways that would never occur to you or me.

Is someone troubling you? Are you feeling indignant, maybe even a little self-righteous? Would you feel justified to expose the person as the evil fraud you know he is? It is time to wait on God. Trust Him to handle the troubling situation. Do what you know is right, and leave the consequences in God's hands. Vindictiveness is beneath a person with your future. This was true for both Abigail and David. It will be true for you and me as well.

What did David learn by turning when Abigail delivered the Father's rebuke? He learned not to react impulsively, but to wait, look, and listen. The Bible says, *"Turn at my rebuke; surely I will pour out my spirit on you; I will make my words known to you"* (Prov. 1:23). The principle is simple: God pours out His Spirit and wisdom on those who respond to His rebuke. Do you want His Spirit and wisdom?

God's rebuke through Abigail was vital. It turned David's heart back to the Father. If David had not learned to look and listen to the Father before reacting to irritating, offensive people, it could have cost David the kingdom. And what about Abigail? If she had not made the best of a bad situation, focused on God's greater purpose, and waited on God's solutions, she could have missed being a Queen of Israel. Likewise, you and I may miss God's plan for us if we do not wait on God's solutions.

Conclusion

You can be one through whom God speaks to one of His children. He can use you to deliver His rebuke. You do not have to be a super-saint or be problem free to be used by God. He only requires a responsive heart and a willingness to share His truth with others. If you humbly received rebukes, then you will be the most sensitive to humbly restore others with your gracious and wise words (Gal. 6:1).

Like Abigail, you will be useable if you:
- Make the best of a bad situation. Be a problem solver rather than a victim.
- Focus on God's greater purpose. He has one for you and for those you encourage.
- Wait on God's solutions. You never know what God may do.

The bottom line: God uses average people to do His work. Stay close to Him. Maintain a responsive heart. Be willing to humbly speak truth into other believer's lives. God may use you to deliver His rebuke to one of His children.

Chapter 8

THE FATHER'S REBUKE:
A HOME AND CHURCH ACTIVITY

I am acquainted with the second level of chastening. A few times, my experience mirrored David's encounter with Abigail. I did not respond to the Father's eye and He used my wife to deliver His rebuke.

Home

One evening, for example, I was casually flipping channels and my eyes caught a television program that pleased my flesh but grieved the Holy Spirit. My heart was pricked. I knew the Father was looking and I should change the channel, but I did not. My old man was alive to the temptation. A spiritual battle like the one described in Romans 7 raged within me. The apostle Paul said:

[15]I do not practice what I want to do, but I do what I hate. . . . [18]For I know that nothing good lives in me, that is, in my flesh. For the desire to do what is good is with me, but there is no ability to do it. . . . [22]For in my inner self I joyfully agree with God's law. [23]But I see a different law in the parts of my body, waging war against the

law of my mind and taking me prisoner to the law of sin in the parts of my body (Rom. 7:15b, 18, 22-23 HCSB).

The battle was raging and my flesh was winning. I did not turn my eyes to the Lord. My eyes thirstily drank in the evil. Since I did not respond to the first level of chastening, the Father was gracious and moved to the second.

My wife walked in, saw what I was watching, and verbalized the truth I was ignoring. "You shouldn't be watching that," she said.

I was caught and convicted. I heard the Father's rebuke through my wife. Her brief but firm rebuke gave me the inner strength I needed to turn off the lust-feeding television program.

Our home life is a vital part of our spiritual growth. Maybe that is a prime reason the world, the flesh, and the Devil has launched an all-out assault on Biblical marriage and family life in modern times.

Never has there been a time in history where, in the privacy of our homes, we can gorge our flesh with lustful cravings by flipping a channel or opening an evil web site on our computers. Confidential polls reveal that the majority of men in our churches regularly visit porn sites. Many women do so as well. The Father's heart is grieved when we ignore His eye and His rebuke. If we do not respond, if we do not guard our eyes and minds, we will experience the Father's rod.

I am convinced that the majority of the rampant infidelity in the church takes place because we fail to respond to the Father's chastening. Our faithful God made a way of escape (1 Cor. 10:13). When He rebukes our fleshly behavior, we can turn to Him. Many marriages can be saved. Many pastors can spare their churches great pain and confusion.

Church

God also speaks through the church. We may hear His rebuke through a pastor's sermon, a Bible-teacher's lesson, or a fellow church member's comment. Whatever the source, the rebuke will confirm what the Holy Spirit has already said in our hearts.

Chastening is one reason the church, the "body of Christ," is vital to our spiritual health. Each of us is related to the Head—Jesus Christ (Eph. 1:22-23). Through Christ we are related to all other believers. God made us interdependent. We need each other. Each of us needs the church. As David heard God through Abigail, we hear God through other members of

Christ's body. When God speaks through your church, do you listen or argue? Are you responsive or resistant?

Home and Church

Sometimes the best way to explain a truth is to show it in action. Consider a pastor's helpful testimony. Notice how the Father used his home and church to chasten him when he chose a self-destructive path.

*****

My name is Shep Bevis.[40] In 2006 I allowed spiritual pride, the worst form of pride, to enter my life. Paul Tripp observed, "Because we are all tempted to be self-sufficient and to think that we are independently righteous, we are all attracted to overinflated, aggrandized views of ourselves. To use Paul's words, we think of ourselves 'more highly than we ought to think' (see Rom. 12:3)."[41] He could have been writing about me. I became a pride-filled pastor, preacher, and man. I had an overinflated, aggrandized view of my importance, and a deflated view of God's importance. As a result, I battled a growing anxiety.

Anyone who imagines God's kingdom will collapse without his gifted ministry creates his own anxiety. I did not know how God managed before I came along, but I was certain He could not manage without me now. I knew He was lucky to have me in His service, but the burden became overwhelming. My inflated ego weighted me down; it was a burden too big to bear.

What do you do with anxiety created by an inflated ego? I can tell you what I did and did not do. I did not turn to the Lord. I did not seek help from other pastors. I was not even open and honest with my wife. I did not humble myself to God. I did not confess and repent of my pride. I did not follow the path to spiritual wholeness. Instead, I began to self-medicate.

One who is called to preach wants to preach to as many people as possible. This had been my dream, and now it was being fulfilled. Along with pastoring my church, I had a growing opportunity to preach multiple

---

[40]Shep Bevis was the Pastor of Trinity Baptist Church in Niskayuna, New York, where my co-author, Timothy K. Christian, is a member. He shared this testimony with Dr. Christian during the spring of 2013. As this book went to the publisher, he was Associate Pastor of the growing and dynamic Gate City Baptist Church, in Jamestown, North Carolina. His testimony is here printed by permission.

[41]Paul David Tripp, *Dangerous Calling: Confronting The Unique Challenges of Pastoral Ministry* (Wheaton: Crossway, 2012), 155.

revival meetings and speak to multiple student groups on various college campuses. Unfortunately, I proved untrustworthy. Instead of being humbled by my opportunities, I became proud of myself. I abused God's gifts and calling. Spiritual pride turned my strength into my greatest weakness.

I developed a destructive pattern. After preaching at my church or at a revival meeting or on a college campus, I would self-medicate as soon as possible. Several times I left a church or college campus, and immediately headed to a convenience store and bought several alcoholic beverages. I never intended to get drunk; I just wanted to escape my anxiety.

Evenings at home were no better. I could not drink alcohol without my wife, Amanda, discovering my secret, so I took anything I could find to help me relax—the stronger the better. Sometimes I took my daughter's sinus medication, sometimes Tylenol PM or Benadryl. But nothing was strong enough to escape God's chastening hand. I simply added guilt to my anxiety.

The preaching, pride, anxiety, self-medication pattern went on for several months. I ignored God's eye and turned a deaf ear to His rebukes. I despised God's chastening. I preached to others but I did not preach to myself.

Finally, one night, after preaching at a South Carolina Baptist Associational Revival, I faced reality. I admitted to myself that I was a fake, a phony, and my life was a veneer. When I got in my car I did not head for a convenience store. Instead, I decided I was not going to live that kind of life anymore. I was either going to live for Jesus or get out of the ministry.

I went home and was honest with my wife for the first time in several months. Amanda was shocked. She had trusted me and I had abused her trust. She had no idea what had gone on in my life. I am sure she sensed that I was turning into a different person, but she had no idea I had become a professional self-medicator.

After I told my story to Amanda, we decided to call, Perry Boulier, a close friend who lived in our town. He is also a family friend and a faithful man of God. I confessed my sinful pattern to Perry, at least as far as I understood it at the time. He wisely took me to the home of Dr. Mike Hamlet, Pastor of the First Baptist Church, North Spartanburg, South Carolina. I put my life and ministry in their hands that night. They decided to take me to Faith Home, a Christian alcohol and drug rehabilitation center in Greenwood, South Carolina. The decision was made on a Monday night, and by Wednesday the details were worked out. I was admitted to Faith Home. That same Wednesday night, Dr. Hamlet went to

New Life Baptist Church in Union, South Carolina, where I was pastor, and resigned for me.

I spent several weeks at Faith Home. To be honest, it was one of the best times in my life, but it did not start out that way. In fact, the first night I was there, my pride rose up in protest.

Faith Home was not the plush place I expected. I thought I was headed to a resort-like rehab clinic for stressed professionals. I imagined a luxury hotel with room service. Instead, I discovered I had been admitted to a rustic, working farm. There was room service, but I was it.

The next morning, Thursday, I called Amanda. "Come get me," I said. "I don't belong here. This is a place for derelicts, drunks, and druggies. I'm a pastor. I'm Shep Bevis, a preacher in demand. I don't need to be here. I'll be fine if you'll come and take me home."

Amanda has always been a godly wife who cared for me and followed my leadership. That day she did the hard thing. She did what I needed, not what I wanted. She said, "No. You have to stay. I'm not coming to get you." And she didn't.

Leaving me at Faith Home was the wisest, most loving thing a wife ever did for her husband. For the first time in many years I was able to just be Shep, be a real person, not a fake. I did not have to put on a mask and pretend to be a pastor one moment and someone else the next. For the first time in a long time I opened myself up to allow others to care for me and love me just for who I really am.

My job assignment at Faith Home was the most life transforming of my activities. It quickly deflated my ego. After the meals, the table scraps were dumped into a large trashcan. I was responsible for loading the trashcan on the back of a pickup truck and driving about a mile to what they called the back 40. There it was my privilege to feed the table scraps to the Faith Home hogs. One day, as I worked, it hit me, "I am the prodigal son. I'm living that story. I'm the proud son who ran away from his Father. He has sent me here to get my attention. He is waiting for me to return home, even though I'm not worthy to be called His son."

At Faith Home I finally allowed the Holy Spirit to examine my heart. I did serious business with Jesus. He worked on me, instead of me focusing on the congregation or preparing another sermon. During that time I confessed my sins, repented and returned to the Father.

I left Faith Home with the realization that God was getting along fine before I came on the scene, His work will go on when I am gone, and He can manage quiet nicely without me now. God was never privileged to have me as His prodigy; I was privileged to be His servant. I was a changed man, but I was sure my sin had sabotaged my future.

At that point, I considered myself damaged-goods. I decided I could not return to the ministry. Why would a church want me? Who wants a pastor who has just checked out of a drug and alcohol rehabilitation center? A new career seemed to be the only option.

Amanda and I sent out resumes and we asked God to provide a job that would meet our family's needs. An interview with a technology firm in South Carolina resulted in a job offer to sell sound and video equipment to churches. All things considered, it seemed to be an ideal position for me. However, when the secretary placed the contract on the table for me to sign, something strange happened. I felt as if all the air had left the room. I could hardly breathe. I began to perspire profusely. I looked across the table at the secretary, and said, "I'm sorry. I can't explain it, but I can't take this job."

As I drove home I wondered how I would explain my decision to Amanda. It was difficult because I could not explain it to myself. Amanda was waiting when I entered the house. I asked her, "Who am I? What does God want me to do?"

At first she would not answer, but I was persistent. "Who am I? What does God want me to do?"

Finally Amanda said, "Shep, you are a preacher. God called you to preach. He wants you to be a pastor."

At that point I contacted a deacon at New Life Baptist Church where I had been the pastor. A couple of nights later some of the church leaders came to our home. They sat on the den floor with me. One of those godly men said, "Shep, have you ever thought that God may have sent you to our church so that we could minister to you now, instead of you ministering to us."

As unbelievable as it may seem, they took me back as their pastor. I have never heard of a church doing anything like that. They spent the next four years restoring me to ministry.

I am now a changed man; I'm a different person. I now know it is not about me. It is about Jesus. I also know how dangerous it is when a person allows pride to enter his or her life. In my case, it was what I consider to be the most dangerous form of pride—spiritual pride.

God's work in my heart resulted in a major attitude adjustment. Today I can say with King Nebuchadnezzar of Babylon, "*He is able to humble those who walk in pride*" (Dan. 4:37 HCSB). My life was transformed through God's chastening. I pray that I will never forget the beautiful road He took me down when He humbled me and deflated my inflated ego at Faith Home.

Chapter 9

A RESPONSIVE HEART
IS MERCIFUL

Now no chastening seems to be joyful for the present,
But painful; nevertheless, afterward it yields
The peaceable fruit of righteousness
To those who have been trained by it
(Hebrews 12:12).

The plush carpet in our living room was a tempting wrestling mat for our boys. Jeremy and Matt knew the family rule, "Do not wrestle in the living room." Generally they obeyed, but not always.

One day I heard Jeremy and Matt wrestling in the living room. I gave them the father's look. They glanced at me and kept on wrestling. I responded with the father's rebuke. They heard, but continued wrestling. I repeated the rebuke more sternly, "Boys, I told you not to wrestle in the living room." Still they ignored me. A third time I said, "Listen, if you don't stop wrestling right now, I'll spank you." They were enjoying their wrestling match more than they were concerned about my warning. They continued wrestling.

After the third warning, I had no choice. We had reached the third level of chastening. I stopped the wrestling match and fulfilled my promise.

When our children disobeyed, I tried not to react in anger. I understood that neither dads nor moms are in a position to discipline their children if they cannot control themselves. I followed a process that gave me time to respond calmly and determine the best discipline to accomplish my goals for them. If a spanking was necessary, I explained the reason to the children. After the spanking, I comforted them, hugged them and assured them that I loved them. If there were tears, it was not from pain but from their pride being wounded or their attitudes being changed.[42]

How did Connie and I determine our children needed a spanking? Proverbs was a key guide. Let me explain.

Our third level of chastening was aimed at helping our children become wise adults. We knew our children needed a spanking if they acted foolishly. They acted foolishly when they ignored my look and rebuke, for *"fools despise wisdom and instruction"* (Prov. 1:7). Connie and I tried to correct our children when they misbehaved or had bad attitudes because, *"The way of a fool is right in his own eyes, but he who heeds counsel is wise"* (Prov. 12:15, emphasis mine). *"The rod and rebuke give wisdom, but a child left to himself brings shame to his mother"* (Prov. 29:15). We understood that *"foolishness is bound up in the heart of a child; the rod of correction will drive it far from him"* (Prov. 22:15). I can testify that my dad's belt did more than hold up his pants. It drove a lot of foolishness from my life, and I wanted to do the same for my children.

Our spankings were never cruel or abusive; no parent's discipline should be. Our spankings were motivated by love and carefully controlled. God said, *"He who spares his rod hates his son, but he who loves him disciplines him promptly"* (Prov. 13:24). Love does not withhold the opportunity to gain wisdom.

---

[42]Our culture has changed and many parenting "experts" now debate the value or correctness of spankings. [See Appendix 3 for a discussion of the cultural shift.] This is not a book about parenting. I recommend that you read Christian parenting books. I wish I had read more while our children were young. Connie and I never imagined we were parenting experts. Many of our parenting skills were learned from our parents, as well as from on the job training. The Christian culture we grew up in also reinforced our parenting style.

Our parents made mistakes and we did as well. But I would not trade my parents' disciplinary style for anyone else's. The way Dad disciplined me worked on me. We hoped similar methods would be effective for our children. I had friends whose parent's screamed at and cursed them. That was not part of my family's lifestyle, and I am thankful.

When it came to spanking, my father's belt across my jean-covered rear end was a safe and effective method of changing my behavior. It briefly stung enough to get my attention, but was not severe enough to be painful or bruise. My dad said that his spankings hurt my pride more than my rear end. He was right. Almost everyday I experienced more pain, bumps, and bruises by playing sports with my friends, than I ever received from my dad's belt. Sports were a lot more fun, but I gained much wisdom and self-control via my father's old belt.

The idea of associating child abuse with the type of spankings I received never crossed my mind. In fact, it would have been child abuse if my father had not taken the time to lovingly discipline me. The only permanent marks that my father's discipline left on me was a mark of the highest love and respect for my parents.

Finally, we disciplined our children for their own protection. The wisest man on earth said, *"Chasten your son while there is hope, and do not set your heart on his destruction"* (Prov. 19:18).

I did not enjoy spanking my children. I finally understood why my Dad said, "This is going to hurt me more than it hurts you." In fact, I often repeated my mentor's very words when I disciplined my children.

Like my dad, I only spanked when all other effective means of discipline were exhausted. Our children learned that my looks and rebukes were serious, and they usually responded. When the first and second levels of discipline were sufficient, we did not proceed to the third. There was no need.[43]

The Father's Rod

Our heavenly Father, likewise, only uses the third level of chastening if we ignore His looks and rebukes. Neither our tears nor our pain give Him pleasure, but He is a faithful Father. He uses the rod if we are foolish. He chastens because He is love (1 John 4:8). He chastens for our good. God chastens to make us wise and to develop sensitive hearts in us.

The Father's rod is never comfortable. It may come in different forms. God may use a financial setback, a physical need, or a family problem to get our attention. Whatever the source, respond wisely. Recognize the Father's rod as an act of love. Do not rebel. Repent.

I am not suggesting, of course, that all problems are because of sin. Neither is all success a certain sign of your purity. If you pause and consider, I have no doubt God will let you know if He is using His rod.

A Responsive Heart

---

[43]There is a time when children are too young to spank, and a time when they are too old. Some spankings are too hard, and some are too soft. Some parents should not spank at all because they cannot control themselves. Other parents should include spankings as one of their disciplinary methods because they have gained the wisdom and experience to know what is best for their child.

When does spanking lose its effectiveness? When I gave my children the choice between a spanking or having to go to bed without watching TV, and they choose a spanking, I knew they were too old for my spankings and other forms of discipline would be more effective.

God's chastening prepared David to lead Israel. When Saul died in battle, David was ready to serve. At last he was able to end his wilderness exile; he moved out of the caves and into Hebron. Saul's forty-year-old son, Ishbosheth, was crowned king in his father's place (2 Sam. 2:8-10), but the men of David's tribe respected God's will more than royal lineage traditions. They gathered in Hebron and crowned David as king over Judah (2 Sam. 2:1-4).

Ishbosheth's reign did not go well. Toward the end of his seventh year, two of the captains in his army, Baanah and Rechab, snuck into his house. They found him in his bed, murdered him, cut off his head and took it to David in Hebron. The captains expected David to be pleased, but they were badly mistaken. David had them executed (2 Sam. 4), thereby making it clear to Israel that he was not behind their crime.

After Ishbosheth's murder, the elders of all the tribes of Israel gathered in Hebron and anointed David as their king (2 Sam. 5:1-3). David was thirty when he became king over Judah and thirty-seven when he became king of all Israel.

David's capital city was in Hebron for seven and a half years. It then moved to Jerusalem, where David reigned for another thirty-three years. In total, David reigned for forty years and six months (2 Sam. 5:4-5). His reign was characterized by multiple military victories and ever-increasing popularity and prosperity.

David's years of chastening in the wilderness were preparation for God's greater purpose. During that season, his heart was fine-tuned to the Father's heart. He grew increasingly sensitive and responsive to the Father's look and voice. As a result, David was a wise and successful king from the beginning of his reign.

God has a greater purpose for you as well. His present activity in your life is preparation for your greater usefulness and fulfillment in the future.

David was a spiritual leader as well as a military and political leader. He pursued God's heart. David was a preeminent prayer warrior, as exemplified in many of his Spirit-inspired Psalms. He was internationally renowned for his instrumental and vocal performances of the Psalms. As "the sweet Psalmist of Israel" (2 Sam. 23:1) he led the nation to worship, trust, and follow the Lord with all their hearts. The shepherd-boy, son of Jesse, became the shepherd of the nation, and God's supernatural favor was on the nation. David fulfilled God's greater purpose for his life.

Commendable Character: Hesed
(Kindness/Mercy) in the Heart

David was a merciful king. Two vignettes highlight his commendable character. The first is in 2 Samuel 9.

Mercy for Mephibosheth

When David's kingdom was established, he sought for members of Saul's family. It was a common practice in that day for kings to eliminate the heirs of a predecessor, lest they lead an insurrection. David discovered that Mephibosheth, Jonathan's son, was alive, and called him to his court.

Mephibosheth was five years old when the Philistines defeated Israel in a devastating battle. Saul and his three sons, Abinadab, Malchi-shua, and Jonathan, were killed (1 Sam. 31:1-6). Mephibosheth's nursemaid assumed the young prince was in danger and ran with him. In the panic he fell, apparently breaking his back and severing his spinal cord. His legs were permanently crippled (2 Sam. 4:4).

Mephibosheth grew up in exile, living at Machir's home in Lo Debar (2 Sam. 9:3-4). Mephibosheth's summons to Jerusalem was a long expected and dreaded message. He thought the King was his enemy and out to get him, but when he entered David's throne room, a great surprise greeted him. He was welcomed and honored rather than condemned to death. *"David said to him, 'Do not fear, for I will surely show you kindness* [hesed] *for Jonathan your father's sake, and will restore to you all the land of Saul your grandfather; and you shall eat bread at my table continually'"* (2 Sam. 9:7). David blessed Mephibosheth to honor Jonathan, restored Saul's land to him, assigned servants to farm the land for him, and gave Mephibosheth a permanent seat at the royal table. From then on Mephibosheth lived in Jerusalem, prospered, and daily ate with the king. David's "kindness," his mercy, was an exemplary act of *hesed*—the Hebrew word for mercy, loving-kindness (especially as extended to the lowly, needy and miserable).[44]

Mephibosheth and Me

---

[44]F. Brown, S. R. Driver, and C. A. Briggs, *Enhanced Brown-Driver-Briggs Hebrew and English Lexicon*, (Oak Harbor, WA: Logos Research Systems, 2000), s.v., חֶסֶד; *"hesed."*

It is easy to see a personal application in Mephibosheth's story. We were crippled by the fall (Gen. 3:1-7). We thought the One who loved us and wanted to show us mercy was our enemy. We lived in our sin-imposed exile, trying to hide from God, when He wanted to welcome us to His table for daily fellowship. At last we were brought into His presence, trembling. When we expected wrath, we were greeted with grace. The Father said, "Do not fear, for I will show you mercy for Jesus' sake." The apostle Paul said, *"For you know the grace of our Lord Jesus Christ, that though He was rich, yet for your sakes He became poor, that you through His poverty might become rich"* (2 Cor. 8:9). God has grace and mercy on sinners for Jesus' sake. We are *"accepted in the beloved"* (Eph. 1:7) and we are glad.

Hesed for Hanun

The second vignette is in 2 Samuel 10. Nahash, the King of Ammon, died. His son Hanun inherited the throne. Ammon was a neighboring kingdom, east of the Jordan River. David had a peace and friendship treaty with Nahash. David wanted to express kindness to Nahash's son, the new king, in his time of grief. His kindness indicated his desire to honor the treaty between Ammon and Israel. *"Then David said, 'I will show kindness [hesed] to Hanun the son of Nahash, as his father showed kindness [hesed] to me.' So David sent by the hand of his servants to comfort him concerning his father"* (2 Sam. 10:2a). David's representatives went to express his *hesed* to Hanun. For the moment, we leave the story there. We will return to it a little later.

Conclusion

A responsive heart is merciful. In other words, the way we treat other people is a clear indicator of how we are responding to God's child training. If our hearts are fine-tuned to the Father's heart, our character will reflect His character. We will be kind and merciful to the lowly, needy, and brokenhearted.

David's mercy and kindness toward Mephibosheth and Hanun displayed his responsive heart. What does your treatment of others tell about your heart?

Chapter 10

A FOOLISH HEART
IS MERCILESS

The Holy Spirit inspired the writer of 2 Samuel to begin chapters 9 and 10 with vignettes that demonstrated David's commendable character. He was merciful to Saul's grandson, Mephibosheth, and to a neighboring King, Hanun. "In both narratives David is shown expressing compassion and generosity toward individuals from the region of Gilead whose royal forebears had recently died."[45] David was merciful to the men when they were vulnerable.

And that is why David's actions in 2 Samuel 11-12 are shocking. He who reigned with exceptional wisdom acted exceptionally foolish. His responsive heart became a hard heart. The merciful king became merciless. David's insight is helpful.

I think the writer has his reasons for placing these two portraits of David-in-his-*hesed* before us. . . . The writer shows us these two glimpses of David in order to form a foil against which to see the David of chapters 11-12. Here [chapters 9-10] is David acting kindly and loyally, there [chapters 11-12] is David throwing kindness and loyalty to the winds. Here is David controlled by his covenants and

---

[45]Robert D. Bergen, *1 and 2 Samuel* in *The New American Commentary*, vol. 7 (Nashville: Broadman & Holman Publishers, 1996), 357.

70

memories, there is David driven by his glands and his secrets. Here David spares and mourns life; there he tramples and destroys life.[46]

David became a merciless king (2 Sam. 11-12). Foolishly, he ignored the Father's look and rebuke.

Second Samuel 11 and 12 confront us with an uncomfortable reality. If David's responsive heart became a hard heart in a short period of time, so can ours.

Springtime in Jerusalem

The story opens with the sun shining, birds singing, and warm wind blowing softly. Winter is over. Spring has come. Life is moving into high gear. Spring is the time to finish business put on hold when winter set in. *"It happened in the spring of the year, at the time when kings go out to battle, that David sent Joab and his servants with him, and all Israel; and they destroyed the people of Ammon and besieged Rabbah. But David remained at Jerusalem"* (2 Sam. 11:1). This is an introductory, summary statement. What David did when he stayed in Jerusalem is unfolded in some detail in the rest of chapters 11 and 12. A few details about Joab's conquest of the Ammonites are given as well.

"Wait a minute," someone says. "You just said David demonstrated *hesed* by sending a sympathy delegation to Ammon. If that is so, why did he send Joab to destroy them?" Great question. Again, the context is vital.

The Previous Fall

When David sent the sympathy delegation to young King Hanun (2 Sam. 10:1-2), his mercy was misjudged. David's delegates were accused of being spies, abused, and sent away humiliated.

[2] . . . David's servants came into the land of the people of Ammon.
[3] And the princes of the people of Ammon said to Hanun their lord, "Do you think that David really honors your father because he has sent comforters to you? Has David not rather sent his servants to you to search the city, to spy it out, and to overthrow it?" [4] Therefore Hanun took David's servants, shaved off half of their beards, cut off their garments in the middle, at their buttocks, and sent them away (2 Sam. 10:2c-4).

---

[46]Dale Ralph Davis, *2 Samuel: Looking on the Heart* (Ross-shire, Scotland: Christian Focus Publications, 1999), 111.

The Ammonites' blunder was monumental, and they soon realized it. *"They saw they had made themselves repulsive* [a stink[47]] *to David"* (2 Sam. 10:6a), but they did not respond wisely. They did not try to make amends. Instead, they hired 33,000 Syrian mercenaries and declared war on Israel (vv. 6b, 8), transforming a misunderstanding into a catastrophe.

David did not wait for the Ammonites and Syrians to invade Israel. He moved onto the offensive. He sent Joab and the army of mighty men to Ammon to meet the aggressors (vv. 7-12). God helped Israel. Joab won a great victory, the Syrians fled, and the Ammonites retreated into Rabbah, their capital city (vv. 13-14).

Finishing the campaign would have required besieging Rabbah, but Joab chose not to do so. Winter was coming. A siege traps people inside a city. No one can come or go. A siege also forces the besieging army to remain camped around the city. So, instead of exposing the army to the winter elements and a shortage of supplies, Joab and his men returned home.

The Syrians, however, did not go home. Following their defeat in Ammon, they regrouped, gathered reinforcements, and intended to invade Israel. David received intelligence of their plan and personally led the entire Israeli army out to meet them at Helam. Scholars are now fairly certain that Helam was a desert region some 30-40 miles east of the Sea of Galilee.[48]

When Israel arrived at Helam, they saw a vast army of infantry, cavalry, and chariots. David attacked without hesitation. A ferocious battle ensued and God gave Israel another great victory. Seven hundred enemy charioteers and forty thousand enemy horsemen were killed. Syria surrendered unconditionally. They became Israel's servants (agreed to pay an annual tribute) and were cured of wanting to help the Ammonites (2 Sam. 10:15-19). Once again David went home a great hero.

Back to Spring

When spring arrived, David sent Joab to finish the Ammonite business. Joab took the mighty men to besiege Rabbah. Spring is a better time for a siege. It is harvest time and Israel's army could feed itself by harvesting the Ammonite's crops. Joab went, *"but David remained at Jerusalem."* Bergen noted:

---

[47]Bergen, 358.
[48]Ibid., 360.

The king's absence from the battlefield at this time should not be understood as dereliction of duty. David had previously remained in Jerusalem when the Ammonites were attacked (cf. 10:7). Furthermore, at some point in David's military career . . . David's men . . . pleaded with him to avoid an active role in military campaigns (cf. 21:17) out of concern for the king's safety and the best interests of the nation.[49]

The Cause

David's absence from the battlefield was not a problem, but the condition of his heart was. A responsive heart can degenerate into a hardened heart. The cause of the change is usually subtle. The change may be so gradual it goes largely unnoticed.

Spiritual Drift

We do not know how it happened; we just know it happened. Somewhere along the way David began to drift spiritually. His heart was no longer tuned to God's heart. He began to turn a blind eye to the Father's looks and a deaf ear to the Father's rebukes. Consequently, he was unprepared for a surprise attack on the palace rooftop.

Surprise Attack

The attack was not by a terrorist who slipped past the secret service. It was far more serious. *"Then it happened one evening that David arose from his bed and walked on the roof of the king's house. And from the roof he saw a woman bathing, and the woman was very beautiful to behold"* (2 Sam. 11:2). As David gazed at the bathing beauty in the buff, the Father looked at David, but David did not notice; he was focused on the "very beautiful" woman. He licked his lips, his heart beat and respiration accelerated, and he turned a deaf ear to the Father's rebuke. The Holy Spirit pricked his heart, "Turn away David," but the King summoned a servant.

Spiritual Abuse

---

[49]Ibid., 364.

David's leadership and administrative gifts were highly developed. He was a skilled strategist accustomed to seeing and solving problems. He saw solutions before others knew there were problems. He could analyze a situation, develop a plan, and deploy the needed personnel to solve the problem. It was David's spiritual gift.

Spiritual gifts can be used or abused. We can use our gifts under the Holy Spirit's control, or we can abuse them in the power of the flesh. Under the Spirit's control, our gifts glorify God and are good for His people (1 Cor. 12:24-25). Under fleshly control, spiritual gifts dishonor God and harm God's people.

On this occasion, David ignored the Father's look and rebuke. He used his gifts in the power of the flesh. *"So David sent and inquired about the woman* [he inquired when he should have ignored]. *And someone said, 'Is this not Bathsheba, the daughter of Eliam, the wife of Uriah the Hittite?' Then David sent messengers, and took her; and she came to him, and he lay with her, for she was cleansed from her impurity; and she returned to her house"* (2 Sam. 11:3-4). David analyzed the situation, devised a plan, and deployed the personnel to carry out his plan. He used his spiritual gifts to facilitate his sin.

Blind Eyes—Deaf Ears

David should have seen warning flags and heard trumpet alerts in his servant's report. He could have responded to any one of three rebukes, but he ignored all three.

First, David ignored God's law. He knew the seventh commandment, *"You shall not commit adultery"* (Ex. 20:14). He knew the tenth commandment, *"You shall not covet your neighbor's wife"* (Ex. 20:17). David was married and he knew Bathsheba was married. Fueled by lust, he turned a blind eye and deaf ear to God's commands. Polygamy was tolerated in ancient Israel, but David was not thinking of a meaningful relationship. He was out to satisfy his libido through the sexual conquest of a very beautiful woman.[50]

---

[50]Bad fruit in the present can normally be traced to bad seeds in the past. God's original plan for marriage was one man and one woman. For a husband to have multiple wives and/or concubines, rather than resisting the lust of the flesh and eyes, weakens a man and makes him more susceptible to infidelity. One man with one woman in his heart is God's original plan. David's multiple wives did not help him overcome temptation: it made him more vulnerable to temptation.

Jesus' words are the standard for those desiring a pure heart-relationship with God: "But I say to you that whoever looks at a woman to lust for her has already committed adultery with her in his heart" (Matt. 5:28). David should be a warning to us

David was well versed in God's law. When an Israeli king began his reign, one of his first God-given responsibilities was to:

> write for himself a copy of this law in a book,
> > from the one before the priests, the Levites.
> > > And it shall be with him,
> > > > and he shall read it all the days of his
> > > life,
> > that he may [notice five reasons]
> - learn to fear the LORD his God and
> - be careful to observe all the words of this law and these statutes,
> - that his heart may not be lifted above his brethren,
> - that he may not turn aside from the commandment
>   > to the right hand or
>   > to the left, and
> - that he may prolong his days in his kingdom, he and his children in the midst of Israel (Deut. 17:18-20).

David knew God's commandments, but he ignored God's commandments. He was without excuse.

Second, David disgraced God's greater purpose for his life. We noted that God commissioned David to be Israel's shepherd-king. As such, he was to protect his subjects, not abuse them for his own ego and pleasure. Bathsheba was "the daughter of Eliam." David should have protected the daughter of a subject, but he disgraced both Bathsheba and her father.

Third, David disrespected her husband, Uriah the Hittite. Ignoring this warning was more monumental than it appears at first.

David's army included an elite fighting force called "the mighty men." They were known for their exceptional skills, heroic exploits, and unquestioned loyalty to David.[51] We might compare them to the U.S. Special Forces or Navy SEALs. The mighty men were then at Rabbah with Joab (2 Sam. 10:7). Uriah was one of the mighty men (2 Sam. 23:39; 1 Chron. 11:41).

Each of these facts was the Father's rebuke. Any one of them should have been sufficient. But instead of hearing God's warnings, David saw an opportunity to satisfy his lust. He knew Bathsheba's husband

---

to guard what our eyes look upon. This is why pornography is so dangerous. It plants the seeds of a terrible harvest.

[51]The mighty men were ordinary men who did extraordinary exploits because they reflected the same kind of faith as their mentor, David. One killed 800 men at one time and another killed 300 enemy soldiers with his spear (2 Sam. 23).

would not be home that night. David called for her, used her, and sent her away. The holy act between a husband and wife was reduced to loveless lust and a calloused, ego-boosting conquest. It was a blatant abuse of power.

Temptation—Confess or Cover?

You and I can learn from David's experience, but we cannot self-righteously condemn him. We know what he faced. It is all too familiar. We have battled our own temptations. More times than we would like to admit, we have lost the battle.

We know *"all that is in the world—the lust of the flesh, the lust of the eyes, and the pride of life—is not of the Father but is of the world"* (1 John 2:16). We also know the temptation to blame God or someone else instead of taking personal responsibility for our sins. James warned:

Let no one say when he is tempted, "I am tempted by God"; for God cannot be tempted by evil, nor does He Himself tempt anyone. But each one is tempted when he is drawn away by his own desires and enticed. Then, when desire has conceived, it gives birth to sin; and sin, when it is full-grown, brings forth death (James 1:13-15).

Blaming God, circumstances, or other people for our sin is convenient, but destructive. God never tempts us to sin; He is holy. Nothing within Him responds to sin. We are different. We are drawn toward and enticed by sin like a fish is attracted to bait or an animal is enticed into a trap. Sin solicits. Wickedness woos. Personal experience confirms this fact both for us and for David. When David committed adultery with Bathsheba, he was drawn and enticed, hooked and trapped.

What should David have done after he sinned? What should you and I do when we sin? We should respond to the Father's chastening. We should humble ourselves, confess and forsake our sin. The Bible says, *"He who covers his sins will not prosper, but whoever confesses and forsakes them will have mercy"* (Prov. 28:13). The Bible promises, *"If we confess our sins, He is faithful and just to forgive us our sins and to cleanse us from all unrighteousness"* (1 John 1:9). Forgiveness and cleansing are available because *"the blood of Jesus Christ His Son cleanses us from all sin"* (1 John 1:7).

David turned away from the mercy available to him. He did not confess and forsake his sin. Instead, he tried to cover his sin. In the process, he multiplied his sin.

The Consequences

David got up the next morning and pretended nothing had happened. No doubt his conscience hounded him and the Holy Spirit convicted him.

A few days passed, then a week, then three. Nothing happened. All seemed to be well. David's conscience calmed and his heart became a little harder. Sin deceives us. It deceived David and it will deceive you and me.

Perhaps David comforted himself, saying, "That wasn't so bad. I was worried about nothing. Maybe I shouldn't have done it, but . . . I'm a hard working king. I need a distraction now and then. I deserve it. Who knows—maybe God moved Bathsheba next door, just for me. Besides, I'm always caring for others. It's time I took care of myself; I'm the King."

A few more weeks passed, and then it happened. David's world turned upside down when he opened an innocent looking note that arrived in the morning mail. *"The woman [discovered that she had] conceived; so she sent and told David, and said, 'I am with child'"* (2 Sam. 11:5).

Again the Father rebuked him with this news. David had another opportunity to repent. He could have asked God for forgiveness and for wisdom to know what he should do, but he turned a deaf ear.

Whatever else may happen, unconfessed sin produces a calloused conscience and a hardened heart. Fellowship with the Father is broken when our hearts are no longer in tune with God's heart. So it was for David; so it is for you and me.

The Cover-up

Rather than confessing and forsaking his sin, coming clean with God, himself, and Uriah, David again abused his gifts and authority. Immediately he analyzed the new problem, developed a plan, and deployed personnel to carry out his plan. He used his spiritual gift to cover his sin.

⁶Then David sent to Joab, saying, "Send me Uriah the Hittite." And Joab sent Uriah to David. ⁷When Uriah had come to him, David asked how Joab was doing, and how the people were doing, and how the war prospered. ⁸And David said to Uriah, "Go down to your house and wash your feet." So Uriah departed from the king's house, and a gift of food from the king followed him (2 Sam. 11:6-8).

David's plan was simple. It seemed foolproof. Send for Uriah, ask for a report and give him a three-day pass. Send him home with a romantic dinner. Hormones would do the rest. Glands got us into this and glands will get us out. Problem solved. Or so he thought.

The plan had a fatal flaw. David did not take into account the discipline and faithfulness he had inspired in his mighty men. "*Uriah slept at the door of the king's house with all the servants of his lord, and did not go down to his house*" (v. 9).

The next morning, David saw his plan unraveling. He called Uriah in for questioning.

¹⁰So when they told David, saying, "Uriah did not go down to his house," David said to Uriah, "Did you not come from a journey? Why did you not go down to your house?"

¹¹And Uriah said to David, "The ark and Israel and Judah are dwelling in tents, and my lord Joab and the servants of my lord are encamped in the open fields. Shall I then go to my house to eat and drink, and to lie with my wife? As you live, and as your soul lives, I will not do this thing" (vv. 10-11).

Uriah's selfless-faithfulness, compared to David's selfish-faithlessness, was another rebuke from the Father. It was another opportunity for David to repent, but he misused the opportunity. He simply revised his plan.[52]

¹²Then David said to Uriah, "Wait here today also, and tomorrow I will let you depart." So Uriah remained in Jerusalem that day and the next. ¹³Now when David called him, he ate and drank before him; and he made him drunk. And at evening he went out to lie on his bed with the servants of his lord, but he did not go down to his house.

---

[52]The Father's chastening is progressive. The longer we refuse God's rebuke the more severe the Father's rod. Consider Leviticus 26:27-28, "And after all this, if you do not obey Me, but walk contrary to Me, then I also will walk contrary to you in fury; and I, even I, will chastise you seven times for your sins." See also Leviticus 26:18, 21, 24 for the seven-fold increase in the severity of God's chastening.

Obviously David thought, "I've given this guy every possible chance, but he won't cooperate. I didn't want to do it, but he has forced me to use a permanent solution."

Witness and be warned. An unrepentant heart becomes a hard heart. An ignored conscience becomes a calloused conscience. David's *hesed* was gone and his faithful servant was treated like an enemy combatant. In a final insult, David sent Uriah's sealed death warrant in Uriah's hand. He made Uriah the messenger of his own murder.

> [14]*In the morning it happened that David wrote a letter to Joab and sent it by the hand of Uriah.* [15]*And he wrote in the letter, saying, "Set Uriah in the forefront of the hottest battle, and retreat from him, that he may be struck down and die."* [16]*So it was, while Joab besieged the city, that he assigned Uriah to a place where he knew there were valiant men.* [17]*Then the men of the city came out and fought with Joab. And some of the people of the servants of David fell; and Uriah the Hittite died also.* [18]*Then Joab sent and told David all the things concerning the war.*

A few days later, a military courier arrived in the throne room with a report from the front. Joab reported that several soldiers had been killed near the wall of Rabbah. Normally David would have reprimanded Joab for using a tactic that unnecessarily sacrificed Israeli lives. This time things were different because Joab's report included one telling sentence: "*Your servant Uriah the Hittite is dead also.*" David's response was calloused at best. "*Then David said to the messenger, 'Thus you shall say to Joab: "Do not let this thing displease you, for the sword devours one as well as another. Strengthen your attack against the city, and overthrow it." So encourage him'*" (v. 25). You can almost hear the suppressed smile in his voice.

David thought he was in the clear. (Please note the vast difference between being in the clear and being clean before God.) David married Bathsheba, she bore him a son, and the cover-up was complete. Or so it seemed. Second Samuel 11 ends with an ominous note. "*But the thing that David had done displeased the LORD*" (v. 27).

Confessing sin leads to restoration. Covering sin leads to destruction. Is God pleased with the way you have dealt with your sins?

The Confrontation

A year or so passed. David and Bathsheba's shame faded. The flowers on Uriah's grave were long gone. Royal responsibilities and domestic life settled into a normal routine. The war with Ammon was going well.

One day Nathan the prophet, David's pastor, came for a visit. He had a story to tell, and David was glad to hear it. The story reported a problem in the kingdom. David knew Nathan had come to the right man. He was a problem solver. He would assess the situation, devise a plan, and deploy personnel to solve the problem. It was his specialty, his gift.

> *[1] Then the LORD sent Nathan to David. And he came to him, and said to him: "There were two men in one city, one rich and the other poor. [2] The rich man had exceedingly many flocks and herds. [3] But the poor man had nothing, except one little ewe lamb which he had bought and nourished; and it grew up together with him and with his children. It ate of his own food and drank from his own cup and lay in his bosom; and it was like a daughter to him. [4] And a traveler came to the rich man, who refused to take from his own flock and from his own herd to prepare one for the wayfaring man who had come to him; but he took the poor man's lamb and prepared it for the man who had come to him"* (2 Sam. 12:1-4).

From our perspective, Nathan's parable was transparent. David was the subject; he was the rich man. Uriah was the poor man and Bathsheba was the precious lamb. David had many wives. Uriah had only one. David used Bathsheba and Uriah for his own pleasure and protection without pity for either.

To us, the meaning is crystal clear. But David missed the point. *"So David's anger was greatly aroused against the man, and he said to Nathan, 'As the LORD lives, the man who has done this shall surely die! And he shall restore fourfold for the lamb, because he did this thing and because he had no pity'"* (vv. 5-6). With this, David passed sentence upon himself.

David soon received four justly deserved strikes from the Father's rod. David had to face the consequences of his sins. *"Do not be deceived, God is not mocked; for whatever a man sows, that he will also reap"* (Gal. 6:7).

If we cover our sin instead of confess our sin, our eyes are blind to the Father's eye. Our ears are deaf to His rebukes. We do not see ourselves in God's Word or hear our needs in His invitation. When we should be humble and repentant, we are self-righteous and judgmental. Our hearts harden.

So it was with David. Where he was previously harsh on himself[53] and filled with *hesed* towards other, he was now easy on himself and harsh toward others. A family pet is valuable to a family, but not worth a man's life. The punishment did not fit the crime.

After listening to the tirade, *"Nathan said to David, 'You are the man!'"* (v. 7a). God sent Nathan to explain why David was about to experience the Father's rod. He had reached the third level of chastening. Nathan continued:

> [7]*Thus says the LORD God of Israel: "I anointed you king over Israel, and I delivered you from the hand of Saul. [8]I gave you your master's house and your master's wives into your keeping, and gave you the house of Israel and Judah. And if that had been too little, I also would have given you much more! [9]Why have you despised the commandment of the LORD, to do evil in His sight? You have killed Uriah the Hittite with the sword; you have taken his wife to be your wife, and have killed him with the sword of the people of Ammon. [10]Now therefore, the sword shall never depart from your house, because you have despised Me, and have taken the wife of Uriah the Hittite to be your wife.' [11]Thus says the LORD: 'Behold, I will raise up adversity against you from your own house; and I will take your wives before your eyes and give them to your neighbor, and he shall lie with your wives in the sight of this sun. [12]For you did it secretly, but I will do this thing before all Israel, before the sun'"* (vv. 7b-12).

The Confession

David was thunderstruck. God had his attention at last. He abandoned his futile attempt to cover his sin—*"David said to Nathan, 'I have sinned against the LORD'"* (v. 13a). The confession was brief because David was broken.

An honest, humble confession does not require a flowery speech. People may be impressed with pious platitudes. God is not; He knows our hearts.

---

[53]His heart smote him when he cut off the corner of Saul's robe (1 Sam. 24:5).

The Restoration

The Father is full of grace and ever willing to forgive repentant sinners. Nathan said, *"The LORD also has put away your sin; you shall not die"* (v. 13b). (Death would have been the fourth level of chastening if David had not repented.) Nathan continued, *"However, because by this deed you have given great occasion to the enemies of the LORD to blaspheme, the child also who is born to you shall surely die"* (v. 14). And so he did, in spite of David's fasting and prayer. The child's death (vv. 15-23) was the first of four blows from the Father's rod (2 Sam. 13-18).

While chastening is not punishment for our sin, it is related to our sin. David killed Uriah with the sword and he was chastened with the sword. David took another man's wife. His son, Absalom, took some of his wives (2 Sam. 16:22). David sinned in secret but God chastened him in public.

David was the leader of the nation. God gave him much and required much from him. David's chastening was a public example and warning to God's people. It is a warning to you and me.

Even so, David's chastening is encouraging. The Father did not abandon David. He never abandons one of His children. He will not abandon you.

David experienced God's mercy in the midst of his chastening. Bathsheba had another boy, Solomon, and Nathan visited with another message from God. This time it was good news. The prophet who previously brought the message of God's judgment now delivered a promise of God's grace.[54] Nathan told David and Bathsheba that God had given Solomon another name, Jedidiah, which means *"beloved of the Lord"* (vv. 24-25). Further, the siege at Rabbah was finally successful. Joab sent word, and David went to Rabbah to accept the Ammonite's surrender (vv. 26-31). David experienced God's grace and goodness even while he endured the Father's rod.[55]

---

[54]Eugene H. Peterson, *First and Second Samuel* (Louisville, KY: Westminster John Knox Press, 1999), 188.

[55]Below we will see the six responses people make to God's chastening. One of the negative responses is to be discouraged. Yet, God said, "Do not faint or be discouraged." Why? We can trust God's grace. Who would have guessed that from this marriage that began as an adulterous affair followed by a murderous cover up, God would raise up Solomon? God loved Solomon, chose him to be king after David, and inspired him to write three books of the Bible. This should give all of us a reason to hope, even if we, like David, have sinned a great and grievous sin.

The Cleansing

God cleanses our sins when *"we confess our sins"* (1 John 1:9). Please notice that forgiveness depends on the sacrifice of our Savior, not on the intensity of our confession. *"The blood of Jesus Christ His Son cleanses us from all sin"* (1 John 1:7). Therefore, when you confess your sin, do not focus on your confession or your sin. Focus on Jesus Christ. Trust Him alone for forgiveness.

David did. Later he spelled out his confession in Psalms 32 and 51. He put on paper what previously was in his heart. Lest anyone think he was comfortable during the year he tried to cover his sins, David wrote, *"When I kept silent, my bones grew old through my groaning all the day long. For day and night Your hand was heavy upon me; my vitality was turned into the drought of summer"* (Ps. 32:3-4). "David describes how it felt to be relentlessly dogged by guilt. . . . The sense of being prematurely old, constant groaning, the feeling of heaviness, the sense of being spiritually parched and destitute—all are the handiwork of guilt."[56]

David's guilt was lifted only when he confessed. Fresh joy flooded his soul as he remembered, *"I acknowledged my sin to You, and my iniquity I have not hidden. I said, 'I will confess my transgressions to the LORD,' and You forgave the iniquity of my sin"* (Ps. 32:5). To his praise for forgiveness, David added a promise for God's children. *"For this cause everyone who is godly shall pray to You in a time when You may be found"* (v. 6). Forgiveness is for anyone and everyone who goes to God by faith.

Even so, David did not want us to think either that forgiveness is cheap because it is free, or earned by an eloquent confession. Cleansing is not psychological; it is supernatural. It is based on God's grace and goodness and the gift of His Son. Therefore David prayed:

¹Have mercy upon me, O God, according to Your lovingkindness; according to the multitude of Your tender mercies, blot out my transgressions. ²Wash me thoroughly from my iniquity, and cleanse me from my sin. ³For I acknowledge my transgressions, and my sin is always before me. ⁴Against You, You only, have I sinned, and done this evil in Your sight— that You may be found just when You speak, and blameless when You judge (Ps. 51:1-4).

---

[56]Roger Ellsworth, *Opening up Psalms* (Leominster, England: Day One Publications, 2006), 97-98.

David realized his sin was primarily against God. He did not try to excuse it or explain it away. He confessed his sin to God, and trusted God to remove, wash, and cleanse his transgressions, iniquity, and sin. His faith was in God's tender mercies and loving-kindness. David's confession is a good example for us.

Christian Confession

Consider three facts for Christians. First, when we confess our sins, justice is not ignored. God does not simply overlook sin, excuse sin, or pretend we did not sin. *"The wages of sin is death"* (Rom. 6:23), and Jesus Christ received the wages in our place. Our sin was on Jesus when He died on the cross. He received our punishment. Since He is the infinite God, He endured the sins of the world in a finite period of time. *"For Christ also suffered once for sins, the just for the unjust, that He might bring us to God, being put to death in the flesh"* (1 Pt. 3:18). God forgives all sinners who come to Him for mercy because justice was satisfied in Jesus Christ's sacrifice. Second, sin, any sin, can be confessed to God in honesty, humility, and faith. Third, sin is ever on our conscience until Jesus Christ forgives and cleanses us. Have you confessed your sins?

Conclusion

The third level of chastening, the Father's rod, is required if we ignore the Father's look and rebuke; He chastens us with the consequences of our sins. We reap what we sow. However, believers do not experience God's condemnation. *"There is therefore now no condemnation to those who are in Christ Jesus"* (Rom. 8:1a). Christians are chastened by the consequences of our sins, but we are not condemned for our sin. In contrast, lost people experience the consequences and the condemnation for their sins, but they are not chastened. Their hearts are not drawn to the Father's heart.

Such was David's experience, and it will be ours as well. Chastening finally got David's attention and he confessed his sin. Confession guarantees cleansing for God's children because of Jesus' sacrifice (1 John 1:7). Grace is a free gift because Christ paid the full price for us.

So, how can we respond to chastening? What steps do we take to get in on grace? Paul answered the question in 1 Corinthians 11. Some members of the church at Corinth were being chastened. They had abused the Lord's Supper. The abuse had gone so far that a few of their members experienced the third level of chastening, and some the fourth. Paul said, *"For this cause many **are** weak and sickly among you* [the Father's rod], *and many sleep* [the Father's final call]. *For if we would judge ourselves, we should not be judged. But when we are judged, we are chastened of the Lord, that we should not be condemned with the world"* (1 Cor. 11:30-32, emphasis mine).

God says, "Judge yourself." Agree with God about your sin. Stop the sin and confess, "Lord, I have sinned. Forgive me. I turn from my sin to Jesus. I trust your mercy and grace. I trust Jesus' blood to cleanse me from all my sins." He promises, *"If we confess* [agree with God about] *our sins, He is faithful and just to forgive us **our** sins and to cleanse us from all unrighteousness"* (1 John 1:9, emphasis mine).

What can you do to receive grace and forgiveness when you are chastened? Confess your sins, trust His forgiveness, and say thanks.

Chapter 11

GOING HOME EARLY

Once upon a time, Thomas and Maria Silvestri invited me to their home. My boys were eight and ten at the time, and went along to spend the afternoon playing with Thomas and Maria's boys.

When we arrived, my boys were a little disappointed. The Silvestri boys were at the mall with their grandparents, but were expected to return soon. Maria knew just what to do. She deposited Matt and Jeremy in their spacious family room to enjoy milk and cookies and Bugs Bunny cartoons.

With my boys happily occupied, Thomas, Maria, and I went into their living room. It was decorated with crystal lamps, fine china figurines, and newly refurbished antique furniture. Impressive artwork was on the walls. Maria cherished the fragile decorative pieces and furnishings because they were family heirlooms.

Our conversation had just begun when we heard a thump and bump in the family room. Thomas did not seem to notice, but I immediately recognized the sounds. I excused myself and rushed to check on my boys. When I looked into the family room, Matt and Jeremy were wrestling on the floor. They sensed my look and stopped wrestling.

"We know," Matt said. "Don't wrestle in someone else's house. Sorry. We'll stop."

Within five minutes of my return to the living room, we heard a loud crash. This time the three of us ran to the family room. Maria led the way. Their over-stuffed leather couch was turned over backwards, milk and cookies were sprayed across the tile floor, and Bugs Bunny had once again tricked Elmer Fudd into shooting Daffy Duck. My boys were oblivious; they did not notice I was looking at them. The overturned couch had become a wrestling rink, and they were struggling to pin one another.

When I spoke, my sons heard the rebuke in my voice and stopped. "Boys, you can't wrestle here; you know the rules. You're in someone else's home. Straighten this room and clean up what you spilled. If you start wrestling again, I'm going to spank you."

"Sorry Dad," they said. "We forgot. We won't wrestle anymore."

Thomas and I returned the couch to its original position. Maria brought paper towels and a pan of warm water, and gave it to my boys. They were accustomed to allowing children to face the consequences of their actions. As we left the family room, my boys were mopping up the milk and collecting the cookies. I'm pretty sure they ate the ones that landed in the milk.

Forty-five minutes passed without further alarms from the family room. Our conversation was moving toward a meaningful conclusion when we heard the distinct sound of one boy body-slamming his brother onto the coffee table. We rushed into the family room. Jeremy was sitting on Matt's chest. Matt had kicked the magazines off of the coffee table in his struggle to prevent Jeremy from pinning his shoulders to the table. The pan of water and mopped up milk was upside down on the couch.

I do not know if Thomas and Maria approved of spankings. We never discussed it. I do know they were glad I took charge of the situation.

I made both boys sit up and look at me, eye-to-eye. "Boys," I said, "I told you not to wrestle here. You have disrespected our friends' home and disobeyed me. Do you remember my warning?"

"You said you would spank us," Matt said, "but Dad, we're sorry. We won't wrestle anymore."

Jeremy chimed in, "Yea Dad, we're really sorry. We don't need a spanking." Both boys were trying not to cry.

"I'm sorry too," I said, "but I warned you. Now you've forced me to spank you."

Thomas and Maria moved into the kitchen. After the spankings I hugged my sons and dried their tears. I told them that I loved them and forgave them, but I added a final warning. "Boys, I want you to have fun, but you must respect this family room. I can't leave you here for the afternoon if you start wrestling again. I'll have to take you home. Matt, do you understand?"

"Yes, Dad, I understand."

"Jeremy, do you?"

"Yes, Dad, I understand."

By then, Maria had made coffee. We finished our conversation in their kitchen breakfast nook.

I was going to pray for the Silvestri family and leave when we heard a sickening sound. I looked up to see horror on Maria's face. "It was my grandmother's," she whispered. Tears were in her eyes.

Thomas looked from Maria, to me, and back to Maria. His expression said, *No! It can't be.*

Multiple thoughts raced through my mind. The first was, *How much is this going to cost me?* I was sure one of the crystal lamps and a couple of the figurines had shattered, and I dreaded seeing the damage to the antique furniture.

My boys had partially obeyed. They were no longer wrestling in the family room. They had moved their match into the living room.

At that point, only one option remained. I had to take my boys home. My look, rebuke, and rod had been ineffective. We had reached the fourth level of chastening.

* * * * *

I'm happy to say the story above is fictional. You probably noticed it began, "Once upon a time." My boys were never so disobedient or disrespectful that I had to take them home from one of our friend's home.

The fiction illustrates a fact: our heavenly Father is longsuffering, loving, and just when He chastens His children. If we refuse to respond to God's various and repeated forms of discipline, God sometimes takes believers home early. This is called *"the sin unto death"* (1 John 5:16). Do not misunderstand. Believers are eternally secure in Jesus Christ. They still go to heaven, but they go sooner than they would have otherwise. They miss out on God's greater purpose for their lives, and they may lose much of their eternal rewards (1 Cor. 3:15; 5:5).[57]

If we do not heed the Father's look, we hear the Father's rebuke. If we do not respond to His rebuke, we experience the Father's rod. If we continue to refuse correction, we will hear the Father's final call.

Uncomfortable Reality

---

[57]"If anyone's work is burned, he will suffer loss; but he himself will be saved, yet so as through fire" (1 Cor. 3:15). "Deliver such a one to Satan for the destruction of the flesh, that his spirit may be saved in the day of the Lord Jesus" (1 Cor. 5:5).

Some readers are uncomfortable with the subject of this chapter. They feel severe discipline is out of character with a loving God. I understand. So did the writer of Hebrews. He anticipated the emotional struggle and answered it with an appeal to our common sense. He said, *"We have had human fathers who corrected **us**, and we paid **them** respect. Shall we not much more readily be in subjection to the Father of spirits and live?"* (Heb. 12:9, emphasis mine). Our dads corrected us and we respected them. Does not the creator of the universe deserve as much respect as our dads?

Our loving, wise God chastens us for our good. He disciplines us to develop sensitive hearts within us.

Please do not miss the last two words of the question in Hebrews 12:9, *"Shall we not . . . be in subjection to the Father of spirits **and live**?"* The author of Hebrews says we have a choice. We can rebel and die or submit and live.

Rebels bring the fourth level of chastening upon themselves, but there is an alternative. We can choose a different lifestyle. We can respond to God's grace and receive His forgiveness. As the Psalmist said, *"The Lord has chastened me severely, but He has not given me over to death"* (Ps. 118:18).

Wise Solomon understood the fourth level of chastening. He said, *"The fear of the Lord prolongs days, but the years of the wicked will be shortened"* (Prov. 10:27). Prolonged days and shortened years are not the result of healthy verses unhealthy lifestyles alone. They are also the result of our response to God's discipline. Solomon warned, *"Harsh discipline* [the Father's rod] *is for him who forsakes the way, **and** he who hates correction will die* [the Father's final call] *"* (Prov. 15:10).

God is merciful and longsuffering, but He will not allow His children to ignore His rebukes indefinitely. *"He who is often rebuked, **and** hardens **his** neck, will suddenly be destroyed, and that without remedy"* (Prov. 29:1, emphasis mine).

Narrow Escape

God is willing to enforce the fourth level of chastening, though He does not want to. He wants us to turn from our sin, receive His forgiveness, and renew our fellowship with Him. He wants to develop sensitive, responsive hearts in us. The prophet Micah understood this fact and praised God for His mercy. He said, *"Who is a God like You, pardoning* *iniquity and passing over the transgression of the remnant of His heritage? He does not retain His anger forever, because He delights **in** mercy"* (Micah 7:18). Isn't that encouraging?

Earlier we noted that King David narrowly escaped the Father's final call. God sent the prophet Nathan to confront David with his sin (2 Sam. 12:1-7). David's heart had become unresponsive. He had ignored the Father's look and His multiple rebukes. Nathan informed David that he had passed the tipping point and would soon experience the Father's rod. Then David repented. *"David said to Nathan, 'I have sinned against the Lord'"* (v. 13a).

Confession is good. Confession is wise. The Bible says, *"He who covers his sins will not prosper, but whoever confesses and forsakes them will have mercy"* (Prov. 28:13). David confessed and forsook his sin, and God was delighted to be merciful. *"Nathan said to David, 'The Lord also has put away your sin; you shall not die'"* (2 Sam. 12:13b).

David heeded Nathan's warning and received God's mercy. Had David ignored the warning, the story would have a different ending. We know this because of King Asa's story.

Chapter 12

CHASTENING AND A SPIRITUAL AWAKENING

Asa was David's great-great grandson. He was the fifth king in David's royal line. Asa's coronation was 60 years after David's death. The nation changed drastically in those 60 years.

David

King David left behind a nation that was loyal to the Lord. After his detour with Bathsheba, his genuine repentance was evident for all to see. The man after God's heart inspired the nation to pursue God with all their hearts. His Psalms trained the people in fervent prayer, exuberant worship, and singular faith in the one, true and living God. Since everything rises and falls on leadership, the nation had risen to be secure and prosperous under David's reign. God's hand was on the man, and God's hand was on the land. God's blessings were evident for all to see.

In contrast, just 60 years later, King Asa received a nation that was disloyal to the Lord. During David's reign such spiritual decline seemed impossible. So how did it happen?

Solomon

God chose Solomon to be David's successor (1 Chron. 22:7-10; 28:5-6). During David's final days, he proclaimed his son Solomon as king. David did not want his sons battling one another for the throne after his death, and he wanted to be sure God's chosen king was on the throne.

David's priority was loyalty to God. He knew it was the key to his son's success. David prayed at Solomon's coronation, *"Give my son Solomon a loyal heart to keep Your commandments and Your testimonies and Your statues, to do all these things, and to build the temple for which I have made provision"* (1 Chron. 29:19). God answered David's prayer. Solomon began with a loyal heart.

Solomon reigned over Israel for 40 years. He dedicated the first 10 years to building the Lord's temple. Solomon humbly sought the Lord during those early years. His heart was in tune with God's heart. God was pleased and gave young King Solomon unprecedented wisdom and wealth (1 Kings 3:10-13). The nation enjoyed peace and prosperity under his administration (4:20-34). At the temple's dedication, Solomon led the nation in enthusiastic worship (8:22-26). His heart was loyal to the Lord and he prayed for God to enter His temple. Solomon's prayer was answered supernaturally. *"The fire came down from heaven and consumed the burnt offering and the sacrifices; and the glory of the LORD filled the temple"* (1 Chron. 7:1).

All did not remain well, however. No one drifts toward holiness—we do not and Solomon did not. Solomon's spiritual disciplines waned with the passing years. He did not maintain a responsive heart. He began to ignore God's look, became insensitive to God's rebukes, and indulged every desire.

Solomon confessed, *"Whatever my eyes desired I did not keep from them. I did not withhold my heart from any pleasure"* (Eccl. 2:10a). His chief indulgence was beautiful women. He married the most gorgeous women in Israel, as well as many exotic beauties from foreign countries. He also made political alliances by marrying the daughters of foreign rulers. His multiple marriages, especially those to foreign women, displeased God.

[1]But King Solomon loved many foreign women, as well as the daughter of Pharaoh: women of the Moabites, Ammonites, Edomites, Sidonians, and Hittites—[2]from the nations of whom the Lord had said to the children of Israel, "You shall not intermarry with them,

nor they with you. Surely they will turn away your hearts after their gods." Solomon clung to these in love (1 Kings 11:1-2; see Deut. 7:1-4).

God's Word proved true. Solomon did all he could to please his foreign wives and make them feel at home in Israel. He adopted an ecumenical outlook; he built temples for their foreign gods. The temples attracted more worshipers than the queens and the servants from their homelands. Idol worship oozed into Israel via King Solomon's foreign wives. The unintended consequence was a national spiritual decline. Even wise Solomon eventually succumbed to a syncretistic idolatry, *"For it was so, when Solomon was old, that his wives turned his heart after other gods; and his heart was not loyal to the Lord his God, as was the heart of his father David"* (1 Kings 11:4). Solomon's loyalty drifted; his heart became unresponsive to God's voice.

I believe Solomon repented in the final years of his life. The aging king wrote Ecclesiastes to warn against the futility of pursuing fleshly pleasures, rather than seeking God. Unfortunately, it was too little, too late. The damage had been done.

Rehoboam

Solomon died and his son Rehoboam became king. Under Rehoboam, the kingdom divided into rival northern and southern kingdoms. The northern kingdom was called Israel; the southern kingdom was called Judah. David's royal line ruled over Judah. Rehoboam, Asa's grandfather, adopted the syncretistic idolatry of his father, Solomon. Notice the sad spiritual state in Judah during his reign.

[22]Now Judah did evil in the sight of the LORD, and they provoked Him to jealousy with their sins which they committed, more than all that their fathers had done. [23]For they also built for themselves high places, sacred pillars, and wooden images on every high hill and under every green tree. [24]And there were also perverted persons [the sexual staff that serviced the worshipers at the fertility shrines[58]] *in the land. They did according to all the abominations*

---

[58]Dale Ralph Davis, *1 Kings: The Wisdom and the Folly* (Geanies House, Great Britain: Christian Focus Publications, 2002), 168.

of the nations which the LORD had cast out before the children of Israel (1 Kings 14:22-24).

Idolatry ceased to be the shocking, resisted exception in Israel. It became the norm. It was no longer the sin of "those foreign people." Idolatry became an accepted, alternative lifestyle and form of worship in Israel.

Abijah

After 17 years of largely incompetent rule, Rehoboam died. His son, Abijah,[59] Asa's father, became king. He reigned only 3 years. *"And he walked in all the sins of his father, which he had done before him; his heart was not loyal to the Lord his God, as was the heart of his father David"* (1 Kings. 15:3). Further spiritual decline, near financial collapse, and continuous war with Israel dominated Abijah's short reign (v. 6).

Asa

Asa was crowned King of Judah after his father's death. A friend could have said, "Asa, I have good and bad news. The good news: you are KING of Judah. It's good to be the King. The bad news: you are King of JUDAH. You are ruler of war-torn ruins, depressed people, and a collapsed economy. You are master of a royal mess. What are you going to do?"

Wise Beginning

---

[59]Abijah is called Abijam in 1 Kings 15:1-8. "Although it may reflect a popular name for Abijah (2 Chr. 12:16), **Abijam** is a strange name for a king of Judah, as it ties together the Hebrew word for 'Father' with the Hebrew word for 'Sea'—normally a deity of Canaan. It is possible that this name reflects the Canaanite influence that had come even into the royal family this early in Judah's reign. The alternative name Abijah is a standard name of praise to God. It means 'My Father Is the Lord.'" Earl D. Radmacher, gen. ed., *NKJV Study Bible*, 2nd ed. (Nashville: Thomas Nelson, 2007), 547.

As surprising as it may be, Asa rose to the challenge by faith. He reversed the trend of the previous 40 years. This is encouraging. A dysfunctional family does not doom you to repeat the sins of your parents and grandparents. Like Asa, you can go in a new direction. *"Asa did what was good and right in the eyes of the LORD his God"* (2 Chron. 14:2). God's eyes were on Asa and Asa's eyes were on God. He led Judah in a different direction. He turned the nation's focus from their problems to the Lord.[60]

Wise, godly leadership is good for a family, it is good for a church, and it is good for a nation. Judah's national revival demonstrated that fact. The new king's heart was sensitive to God's heart and God's Word. His sensitive heart and firm faith invigorated his bold leadership.

> *[3]He removed the altars of the foreign gods and the high places, and broke down the sacred pillars and cut down the wooden images. [4]He commanded Judah to seek the LORD God of their fathers, and to observe the law and the commandment. [5]He also removed the high places and the incense altars from all the cities of Judah, and the kingdom was quiet under him* (2 Chron. 14:3-5).

Changing Hearts

King Asa had a responsive heart. Most of his people did not. A leader cannot change his people's hearts, but he can create an environment that encourages heart-change. Asa wanted his people to worship the true God instead of false gods, so he destroyed their idols and altars.

King Asa sought the LORD. He commanded the people to seek the LORD and obey His laws and commandments. Asa led Judah down a new path, or more accurately, back to *"the old paths"* (Jer. 6:16). Unlike his father, grandfather, and great grandfather, King Asa did everything in his power to create an environment that was conducive to seeking, worshiping, and obeying the LORD.

---

[60]See the author's book, *Growing Through the Storms of Life*, for a more detailed discussion of how God uses trials in believer's lives to mature their faith. Contact Boca Glades Baptist Church, 10101 Judge Winikoff Rd., Boca Raton, FL 33428, (561) 483-4228, to order your copy.

Changing Habits

Changing a bad habit requires a consistent change of behavior. If one needs supplies to practice a sinful and/or destructive habit, he should destroy the supplies and not purchase more. Also, he should avoid the places that encourage the habit. This is common sense. It is also scriptural. The Bible says, *"Put on the Lord Jesus Christ, and make no provision for the flesh, to fulfill its lusts"* (Rom. 13:14, emphasis mine).

King Asa understood this reality. Do we? Asa removed the idols and destroyed the places where people worshiped the idols. He gave the nation an idol-free environment for the first time in several decades.

No doubt, Asa's reforms were resisted. The Bible does not describe the initial response, but human nature has not changed. Reforming religious practices is seldom popular, even if it is right and true. Idol worship produced significant income for many citizens. Many more were dedicated participants. Removing the idols was unpopular, but it was a bold step of faith. Also, it was best for the people. God was pleased and confirmed Asa's leadership with peace and prosperity.

> *⁶And he built fortified cities in Judah, for the land had rest; he had no war in those years, because the LORD had given him rest. ⁷Therefore he said to Judah, "Let us build these cities and make walls around them, and towers, gates, and bars, while the land is yet before us, because we have sought the LORD our God; we have sought Him, and He has given us rest on every side." So they built and prospered* (2 Chron. 14:6-7).

New construction usually signifies a reviving economy. So it was in Judah. New walled cities were built. The southern kingdom enjoyed 10 years of political peace and economic recovery (14:1). Security and prosperity returned to Judah.

Preventative Maintenance

Security and prosperity are desirable, but they can become a two-edged sword. They can lead to complacency. Complacent people feel superior to their struggling predecessors. The complacent imagine they deserve their exceptional blessings. They feel entitled instead of thankful.

Sometimes God allows trials and storms into our lives to prevent complacency. Storms are not always corrective. Sometimes they are preventative maintenance. They remind us to continue trusting the Lord. God uses storms as child training. Storms can help us maintain responsive hearts.

After 10 years of peace and prosperity, King Asa and his people faced a great storm. An invading army came from Ethiopia with 1,000,000 soldiers and 300 chariots (2 Chron. 14:9).

Again, Asa rose to the challenge by faith. He led his army to face the invaders, but his eyes were on God. He knew God was his source of security. He trusted God for deliverance rather than trusting his ingenuity or expertise.

> *[11]And Asa cried out to the LORD his God, and said, "LORD, it is nothing for You to help, whether with many or with those who have no power; help us, O LORD our God, for we rest on You, and in Your name we go against this multitude. O LORD, You are our God; do not let man prevail against You!" [12]So the LORD struck the Ethiopians before Asa and Judah, and the Ethiopians fled"* (2 Chron. 14:11-12).

When God is working, the outcome of a battle is not dependent on the size of an army or the strength of its forces. God can win with many or few, the strong or the weak. Asa knew this, so he prayed, "Help us. You are our God. We rest on You. We fight in Your name. Protect Your name and reputation."

Asa saw the invasion as an attack on God as well as on Judah. He prayed, *"O LORD, . . . do not let man prevail against You!"* (v. 11d). It is true today as well. An attack on values that are founded in the Bible is not an attack on a bigoted culture. It is an attack on God, on His wisdom about what is best for us, and on His truth. Such attacks call us to pray as Asa prayed.

Asa prayed for God to defend Himself as well as His people. And God did. He used Judah's comparatively small and weak army[61] to strike the Ethiopians' huge and mighty army. The surviving Ethiopians ran away.

---

[61]Asa's 580,000 skilled soldiers (2 Chron. 14:8) were not insignificant. But compared to 1,000,000 skilled soldiers and 300 chariots, Judah's army was weak and small.

Judah collected great spoils and returned to Jerusalem victorious (vv. 13-15).

Faith-Building

The invasion was not chastening for sin. Asa was obeying God when the million-man army attacked. This chastening was faith building. It was child training for future challenges. It was preparation for greater blessings. God wanted to enlarge Asa's influence and increase Judah's wealth, but He wanted them to be spiritually prepared for His blessings. The invasion kept the nation relying on God.

Are you facing a difficult time in your life? Has an unexpected storm blown into your life? Before it came, were your sins confessed. Were you seeking the Lord with all your heart? If so, your storm is not corrective chastening; it is preventative maintenance. It is faith fortifying against future enemy attacks. (If you can trust God now, you can trust Him in the future.) It is preparation for enlargement and for greater usefulness.

Your storm demonstrates your Father's faithful love as He fine-tunes your heart. A storm is your opportunity to draw close to God instead of drifting away from God.

Multiple Blessings

Christians *"know that all things work together for good to those who love God, to those who are called according to His purpose"* (Rom. 8:28). As it is with Christians today, so it was for Asa and Judah. God transformed the Ethiopian crisis into multiple blessings.

Increased Security

First, the Ethiopian invasion increased Judah's security. This is surprising. Who could have predicted an invasion would be the pathway to security? But it was. God's decisive defeat of the million-man army transformed Judah's insecurity into security; their panic into peace. The defeat was so complete that the Ethiopians never threatened Asa again. *"The Ethiopians were overthrown, and they could not recover, for they were broken before the Lord and His army"* (2 Chron. 14:13b). In fact, not only did the Ethiopians not return, none of Judah's neighbors dared threaten her. God's promise was fulfilled. Before the nation entered the Promised Land, Moses said:

> [2] *"And all these blessings shall come upon you and overtake you, because you obey the voice of the Lord your God: . . . [7] The Lord will cause your enemies who rise against you to be defeated before your face; they shall come out against you one way and flee before you seven ways. . . . [10] Then all peoples of the earth shall see that you are called by the name of the Lord, and they shall be afraid of you"* (Deut. 28:2, 7, 10).

Judah was at peace with all the surrounding nations for the next 25 years. *"And there was no war until the thirty-fifth year of the reign of Asa"* (2 Chron. 15:19).

Enlarged Treasury

Second, the Ethiopian invasion enlarged Judah's treasury. Again, surprising. Invaders usually cause poverty instead of prosperity. In this case, the spoils captured in the conflict enriched Asa and the nation. After the battle *"they carried away very much spoil"* (2 Chron. 14:13c). Trusting God gave unexpected rewards. It did then and it does now. You do not know what God may do in your situation if you will trust and obey.

Built Faith

Third, the Ethiopian invasion built Asa and Judah's faith. It was preventative maintenance that drew them close to God and further developed their responsive hearts.

Pleased God

Fourth, Asa's faith-response to the Ethiopian invasion pleased God. He sent a prophet to encourage King Asa and his army. *"Now the Spirit of God came upon Azariah the son of Oded. And he went out to meet Asa, and said to him: "Hear me, Asa, and all Judah and Benjamin"* (2 Chron. 15:1-2a). Azariah gave three encouragements.

➤ God is with us—seek Him. Azariah said, "The LORD is with you while you are with Him. If you seek Him, He will be found by you" (v. 2b).

➤ God answers prayer—trust Him. Azariah continued, "For a long time Israel has been without the true God, without a teaching priest, and without law; but when in their trouble they turned to the LORD God of Israel, and sought Him, He was found by them" (vv. 3-4). God has always dealt with His people in grace.

➤ God rewards faithfulness—obey Him. Azariah concluded, *"But you, be strong and do not let your hands be weak, for your work shall be rewarded!"* (v. 7).[62]

Azariah's message is timely; it applies to us. We can be sure that God is with us, hears us, and rewards our faith and faithfulness. Jesus promised, *"Ask, and it will be given to you; seek, and you will find; knock, and it will be opened to you"* (Matt. 7:7). We can seek Him, trust Him, and obey Him. However, spiritual vigilance is required for us to maintain responsive hearts.

Asa needed spiritual vigilance as well. Azariah's encouragement included the warning: *"If you forsake Him, He will forsake you"* (v. 2c). "More than one general has won a battle but afterwards lost the war because of pride or carelessness, and the Lord did not want Asa to fall into that trap."[63]

God was pleased that King Asa and his army trusted Him in a great crisis. They called and He answered. When you face a crisis, do you call on the Lord or complain about the Lord? Seek Him. Trust His care and faithfulness.

Renewed Cleansing

Fifth, the Ethiopian invasion prompted a renewed cleansing in the southern kingdom.

And when Asa heard these words and the prophecy of [Azariah the son of[64]] Oded the prophet, he took courage, and removed the abominable idols from all the land of Judah and Benjamin and from

---

[62] Warren W. Wiersbe, *The Essential Everyday Bible Commentary* (Nashville: Thomas Nelson Publishers, 1993), 559.

[63] Warren W. Wiersbe, *The Bible Exposition Commentary: History* (Colorado Springs, CO: Victor, 2003), 463.

[64] Marginal note, NKJV.

the cities which he had taken in the mountains of Ephraim; and he restored the altar of the LORD that was before the vestibule of the LORD (2 Chron. 15:8).

Idols were removed from the cities that Judah had just captured. Apparently, some of the idol shrines that were destroyed at the beginning of Asa's reign had been rebuilt. The prophet's words encouraged Asa, and he again cleansed the entire kingdom.

God's Word encourages our purity. Our Lord Jesus prayed, *"Sanctify them by Your truth. Your word is truth"* (John 17:17). "**Sanctify** means 'to set apart.' . . . Jesus was praying not only that the disciples should be kept from evil, but that they should advance in holiness."[65] Through reading, studying, and meditating on God's Word, we are sanctified. We are kept from evil and we grow in holiness. Are you feeding on God's Word daily?

Revival Spread

Sixth, the Ethiopian invasion spread revival to the northern kingdom. When Israel heard what God was doing in Judah, many were drawn back to the Lord. They abandoned their idols and began going to Jerusalem for the annual festivals.[66] They began worshiping the Lord with all their hearts. The spiritual awakening inspired many to migrate to Judah.

[9]Then he gathered all Judah and Benjamin, and those who dwelt with them from Ephraim, Manasseh, and Simeon, for they came over to him in great numbers from Israel when they saw that the LORD his God was with him.

[10]So they gathered together at Jerusalem in the third month, [likely the Feast of Weeks, also known as Pentecost (Lev. 23:15-21)] *in the fifteenth year of the reign of Asa. [11]And they offered to the LORD at that time seven hundred bulls and seven thousand sheep from the spoil they had brought. [12]Then they entered into a covenant to seek the LORD God of their fathers with all their heart and with all their soul; . . . [15]And all Judah rejoiced at the oath, for they had sworn with all their heart and sought Him with all their soul; and He was found by them, and the LORD gave them rest all around* (2 Chron. 15:9-15).

---

[65]Radmacher, 1694.
[66]See Leviticus 23 for a list of the festivals.

Conclusion

The Ethiopian invasion originally looked like an impossible problem. The situation looked hopeless. It appeared that the million-man army would overwhelm Judah. King Asa responded in faith. He asked God to help them. God answered with an amazing victory. What the enemy intended for evil, God intended for good.

God brought multiple blessings out of the Ethiopian invasion. He increased their security, enlarged their treasury, and built their faith. God was pleased, national cleansing was renewed, and revival spread to the northern kingdom. It appeared that reunification of the divided nation might be possible for the first time.

God is still able to bring blessings out of apparently impossible situations; He can still bring a spiritual awakening. What evil the enemy intends to bring into our lives, God can turn into good (Gen. 50:20). God is able to make *"all things work together for good to those who love God, to those who are called according to His purpose"* (Rom. 8:28). I am glad we can trust Him in our trials and storms.

Chapter 13

THE FATHER'S FINAL CALL:
A SURPRISING CANDIDATE

"Shall we not much more readily be in subjection
To the Father of spirits and live?" (Heb. 12:9b)

Following the victory over the Ethiopians, Judah enjoyed 25 years of peace and prosperity. A spirit of revival dominated their worship for many of those years.

Eventually, however, complacency infected Asa's heart. He began to drift spiritually. His heart was no longer as responsive as it had been. His passionate pursuit of God degenerated into semi-formal religious activity. He did not fall into false worship or sinful habits. He simply took God's blessings for granted and began trusting his own ingenuity.

Search your own heart. Does Asa's spiritual condition sound familiar?

Difficulties and crises often turn our eyes toward the Lord. We realize we desperately need God's help; we will be sunk if He does not come through. God uses trials and storms to get our attention.

Good times should also turn our hearts to the Lord in gratitude. We can draw close to Him because we appreciate His goodness. But, sometimes we are not grateful. We take our blessings for granted. Human nature is such that if we are not delighting in the Lord, we are drifting away from the Lord. Asa is an example for us that responsive hearts can become hardened hearts. We can drift from the blessings of obedience into severe chastening for disobedience.

Paul asked, with a bit of amazement, *"Do you despise the riches of His goodness, forbearance, and longsuffering, not knowing that the goodness of God leads you to repentance?"* (Rom. 2:4). Do not misinterpret God's goodness as His approval of, or indifference toward, your sin. His goodness should lead us to repentance. God's goodness and patience should turn our hearts toward Him.

Baasha's Intimidation

Asa's heart needed preventative maintenance once again. God gave Asa another opportunity to seek Him. Since Asa had drifted while basking in the sunshine of His goodness, the Father allowed another huge trial to cast its long shadow over Asa's reign.

In the 36th year of Asa's reign, Baasha the King of Israel determined to stop the pilgrims and immigrants from going to Judah. He wanted to protect his power-base and tax-base by stopping his people's participation in Judah's revival. He wanted to keep them away from worship in the Jerusalem temple.

Baasha's strategy was not new. Preventing temple worship had been a priority of the northern kings since the days of Jeroboam, the first of the northern kings.

> 26And Jeroboam said in his heart, "Now the kingdom may return to the house of David: 27If this people go up to offer sacrifices in the house of the LORD at Jerusalem, then the heart of this people will turn back to their lord, Rehoboam king of Judah, and they will kill me and go back to Rehoboam king of Judah." 28Therefore the king asked advice, made two calves of gold, and said to the people, "It is too much for you to go up to Jerusalem. Here are your gods, O Israel, which brought you up from the land of Egypt!" 29And he set up one in Bethel, and the other he put in Dan (1 Kings 12:26-29).

During Asa's reign, as more and more Israelites abandoned idol worship and went to Jerusalem to worship the true and living God, King Baasha feared that his position, power, and person were threatened. He formulated a plan to stop the revival. He began building the fortified city of Ramah on Israel's extreme southern border, just 6 miles north of Jerusalem. The construction, so near Judah's capital, was intimidating.

"From this outpost he would be able to monitor his own people who might go to Jerusalem and also launch his own attack on Judah."[67]

Asa's Interpretation

Asa interpreted Baasha's building project as a political challenge requiring a political response. He too formulated a plan. Asa took a large amount of gold and silver from the temple treasury and the king's treasury and sent it to Ben-Hadad, the corrupt king of Syria, Israel's northeastern neighbor. Asa bribed Ben-Hadad to break his treaty with Baasha and make a treaty with him. The treaty was profitable for Ben-Hadad. *"So Ben-Hadad heeded King Asa, and sent the captains of his armies against the cities of Israel. They attacked Ijon, Dan, Abel Maim, and all the storage cities of Naphtali"* (2 Chron. 16:4).

Asa's plan worked. Baasha had to abandon Ramah to fight Ben-Hadad. Asa then took the stones and timbers from Ramah and built two fortress cities for Judah: Geba and Mizpah (vv. 5-6).

Likely, Asa was praised for his clever, strategic political maneuver. He had protected his nation, prevented an invasion, and avoided a war without losing a man or firing an arrow. I imagine his pole number skyrocketed and the headlines praised him for his insightful foreign policy. The foreign aid budget had been well worth the investment.

Asa and his administration had plenty to make them proud. He served Judah well, and he increased national security in the process.

Hanani's Interruption

Asa was probably happy when his secretary interrupted the workday to say Hanani the seer was waiting to see him. Hanani did not have an appointment, but Asa was glad he had come. It seems Asa expected another commendation from the Lord, similar to the one Azariah delivered 26 years earlier. However, the warm welcome quickly turned into a chilly reception.

Hanani wounded Asa's pride when he delivered a rebuke instead of a commendation. He said, "Asa, God is not pleased with you. You trusted Syria instead of trusting the LORD. Didn't you learn from your experience with the Ethiopians? A huge army with many chariots and horsemen invaded, and the LORD delivered them into your hand. You trusted God then, why not now? You have acted foolishly and now you

---

[67]Wiersbe, *Bible Exposition Commentary*, 465.

must face the consequences." Hanani noted three consequences Asa brought upon his nation.

Enemy Escaped

First, Judah's enemy escaped. Hanani said, *"Because you have relied on the king of Syria, and have not relied on the LORD your God, therefore the army of the king of Syria has escaped from your hand"* (2 Chron. 16:7). Instead of making a treaty for Ben-Hadad's assistance, he should have offered Ben-Hadad the opportunity to unconditionally surrender Syria's forces. Asa's lack of faith allowed the enemy to escape.

Intervention Missed

Second, Asa missed God's supernatural intervention. God wanted to give Asa something far better than he could imagine. Maybe God was ready to extend the national revival and reunify the kingdom under Asa's authority. At the very least, verse 7 indicates God wanted to give Syria to him.

We do not know what God would have done if Asa had trusted Him. Whatever it was, Asa lost it with his political maneuver. We know he missed seeing God do something incredible because Hanani said, *"For the eyes of the LORD run to and fro throughout the whole earth, to show Himself strong on behalf of those whose heart is loyal to Him"* (v. 9a). God is searching the whole earth for someone with a loyal heart. He is looking for someone who will trust Him with every part of his or her life. He will show His power in that person's life. But Asa missed it. Asa did what he could do (a political maneuver) and missed what God can do (a powerful miracle).

I wonder how many times you and I have missed God's supernatural activity in our lives. God is still searching the earth for people with loyal hearts.

War

Third, God sent war. Hanani said, *"In this you have done foolishly; therefore from now on you shall have wars"* (v. 9b). Asa's political maneuver was intended to avoid war. Instead, his disloyal heart brought wars on the nation.

Solemn Warning

King Asa's response to Hanani's interruption revealed an insensitive heart. He did not receive Hanani's rebuke. Instead, *"Asa was angry with the seer, and put him in prison, for he was enraged at him because of this. And Asa oppressed some of the people at that time"* (v. 10).

Do you get angry and lash out at others when someone tells you an unflattering truth about yourself? If so, it is not a sign of righteous indignation. It is a sign of an insensitive heart. It is a warning that you are drifting away from God. Beware![68]

Asa is a solemn warning for all of God's children. Do not despise the Lord's chastening. Maintain a responsive heart. Asa drifted away from the Father after more than 30 years of faithfulness and blessing. Do not refuse God's varied and repeated chastening. Trust Him in all your trials. They are preventative maintenance for your faith. Rely on Him and feed on His Word. It will sanctify your heart—it will lead you away from sin and you will grow in holiness. Say with the Psalmist, *"It is good for me that I have been afflicted, that I may learn Your statutes"* (Ps. 119:71, emphasis mine).

Four Levels Of Chastening

King Asa's story brings us back to where we began. Asa's life reveals the four levels of chastening. At the end of his life, his heart was no longer responsive to the **Father's look**. When Baasha began building Ramah, Asa did not look to the Father for direction. He devised his own scheme to solve the problem. He trusted a political alliance with a pagan king, rather than trusting in the Lord alone.

Hanani delivered the **Father's rebuke**, but Asa rejected it. He did not repent. Instead, he got angry. Asa's anger boiled over into rage and he

---

[68]Godly King Asa, leader in a national revival, became a scoffer. He hated the prophet Hanani for his rebuke. In contrast David was wise. He loved Nathan the prophet and received God's rebuke from him. "Do not correct a scoffer, lest he hate you; rebuke a wise *man,* and he will love you" (Proverbs 9:8). Asa saw Proverbs 29:1 fulfilled in his own life, "He who is often rebuked, *and* hardens *his* neck, will suddenly be destroyed, and that without remedy."

took it out on others. He imprisoned Hanani and oppressed some of his people.

Next, Asa experienced the **Father's rod.** *"And in the thirty-ninth year of his reign, Asa became diseased in his feet, and his malady was severe; yet in his disease he did not seek the LORD, but the physicians"* (2 Chron. 16:12).

The Father was patient with Asa. Baasha's intimidation was in the 36th year of Asa's reign. Some three years passed. Asa's heart became increasingly insensitive until the Father used His rod; God corrected him with a foot disease, but Asa hardened his heart. He did not seek God's help with Baasha, he did not repent when he was rebuked, and he even refused to ask the LORD to heal his feet. He only sought help from the royal physicians. He did not repent under the Father's rod.

Did God want to hurt his child? No. God chastened Asa to correct and cleanse him. The Father wanted to restore their fellowship, but Asa despised His chastening (Heb. 12:5). The Father had to say, "I have chastened you in vain; you received no correction."[69]

The fourth level of chastening, the **Father's final call,** took his rebellious son home. *"So Asa rested with his fathers; he died in the forty-first year of his reign"* (2 Chron. 16:13). Asa was at least in his 60s when he died, maybe older. We do not know his age when he became king, but we know he went to heaven sooner than he would have otherwise. For the last two years of his life he endured pain and infections in his feet. Instead of enjoying personal and national revival, instead of enjoying fellowship with the Father, he endured one useless, painful treatment after another. He endured it all with a grumpy, self-righteous, bitter, prayer-less attitude. And then he died.

"They buried him in his own tomb, which he had made for himself in the City of David; and they laid him in the bed which was filled with spices and various ingredients prepared in a mixture of ointments. They made a very great burning for him" (v. 14).

Conclusion

Asa died with a good reputation. He was buried with honors and accolades. Even so, he died out of fellowship with the Lord. God had other plans—great plans—for Asa, but Asa failed to finish his mission on earth.

---

[69]"In vain I have chastened your children; they received no correction" (Jer. 2:30a).

The Father took him home early. Asa died because he refused to respond to the Father's loving, wise chastening.

God deals with us individually. When someone is sick, do not assume that person is like Asa, chastened by the Lord. You do not know his or her heart. I can think of at least nine Biblical reasons for sickness and only one is chastening.[70] Sometimes sickness is for the "glory of God" (John 11:4). Sometimes it simply confirms that we live in fallen bodies in a fallen world. It confirms that Genesis 3 is a historical fact; sin brought sickness, suffering, and death into the human race (Rom. 5:14-19). Be careful not to judge others (Matt. 7:1-2).

On the other hand, examine your own heart (Gal. 6:3-4). Ask God about every sickness or trial you face. Pray about everything. Maintain a sensitive, responsive heart. If you are being corrected, the Holy Spirit will put His finger on the area of your life where He is dealing with you. No matter what you discover, receive the Father's chastening. Do not look away from His eye, ignore His rebuke, or despise His rod. Do not resist His chastening. God is ready to forgive, restore, and renew His fellowship with you.

Chastening is not comfortable, but it is always good for us. It is one of the Father's good gifts. Receive and respond to His child training. There is no reason to go home early. Remain responsive; finish your mission. God's purpose is far greater than you can imagine.

---

[70]I heard Manley Beasley give several Biblical Reasons for Sickness. As best as I can remember they were: (1) Living in a fallen, sin-cursed world (Gen. 3:1-19); (2) Inherited ailments (Gen. 5:3); (3) Aging (4) Demonic attacks (Mark 9:25-26); (5) Chastening because of sin (1 Cor. 11:30); (6) Chastening to refine us (Heb. 12:5-11); (7) God's glory (John 9:3; 11:4); (8) Making us weak that we might depend on His strength (2 Cor. 4:7-11); (9) Taking us to heaven (2 Cor. 5:1-4).

Chapter 14

OUR RESPONSE TO CHASTENING

The reality of the four levels of chastening challenges us to answer a simple question: "Now what?" How will we respond to chastening? The examples we observed from Israel's monarchy affirm that, like David, Solomon, and Asa, we can respond to chastening in different ways at different times in our lives. By the way, that is consistent with my responses to my Dad's discipline. I responded differently at different times, and you probably did as well.

How does God want us to respond to chastening? What consistent response can we make? The search for a Biblical answer sends us back to Hebrews 12 where we began this study. The discussion of chastening is in verses 5-11. Notice the context.

Realistic Questions

The writer of Hebrews opened the chapter with a dose of reality. He had just completed the most famous chapter of his book: "God's Hall of Fame," Hebrews 11. The men and women in God's Hall of Fame did not qualify for entrance by their abilities, but by their faith. It is faith that pleases God. In fact, there is no other way to please Him. *"But without faith **it is** impossible to please **Him**, for he who comes to God must believe that He is, and **that** He is a rewarder of those who diligently seek Him"* (Heb. 11:6, emphasis mine).

By faith Abel worshiped God, Enoch walked with God, and Noah worked for God. By faith Israel's patriarchs and matriarchs, Abraham and Sarah, Isaac, Jacob, and Joseph pleased God. By faith Moses and the children of Israel were delivered from Egypt, observed the Passover, and walked through the Red Sea on dry land. By faith the walls of Jericho fell and the harlot Rahab survived to become an ancestor of our Lord Jesus. By faith Gideon, Barak, Samson, Jephthah, David, and Samuel worked righteousness and won great victories for their nation. By faith many other unnamed saints endured and died in poverty, afflictions, and persecutions [Does that sound like *Your Best Life Now?*]—*"of whom the world was not worthy"* (v. 38).[71]

With these testimonies of faith buzzing in our minds, Hebrews 12 begins,

> *"Therefore, since we are surrounded by so great a cloud of witnesses* [the faithful ones in Hebrews 11 are witnesses to the fact that we too can endure trials and please God by faith], *let us lay aside every weight, and the sin which so easily ensnares us, and let us run with endurance the race that is set before us, looking unto Jesus, the author and finisher of our faith"* (vv. 1-2a).

The writer of Hebrews did not look at life through rose-colored glasses. Neither should we. Consider some realistic questions.

Are you facing difficulties, challenges, and hardships in your life? Are you weary or disheartened? If so, why? What is your attitude toward your hardships? Do you look at your problems through eyes of faith?

Troubling Questions

Do you blame God? "Why did God let this happen to me? Doesn't He love me?"

Do you blame others? "Why won't anyone give me a break? It isn't fair. Someone is always on my case."

Do you blame yourself? "What's wrong with me? Where did I go wrong? I never do anything right."

---

[71] Hebrews 11 mentions none of the sins of the faithful. We have God's view of forgiven saints. However, God does record the sins of each Hall of Fame inductee in the Old Testament. Sometimes they walked in the flesh rather than in the Spirit (Gal. 5:16-26). God also records, for our learning, His chastening/child training of several of His faithful, including Abraham, Jacob, Joseph, Moses, and David. Their response to the Father's chastening is recorded as well. They all endured, respected and submitted to the Father, and were trained by His chastening.

Looking for Answers

If life's trials create troubling questions, the answer is not within. Look outside yourself; look to Jesus.[72] *"Consider Him"* (Heb. 12:3).

Jesus Christ suffered far more than you think. He endured the cross and its shame (v. 2).

Jesus' crucifixion-sufferings were spiritual as well as physical. He endured the agonizing, inhuman, searing pain of a Roman scourge and a Roman cross. Worst of all was the spiritual suffering and separation. He *"who knew no sin"* (2 Cor. 5:21) took all of our sins upon Himself. He endured the Father's holy wrath against the sin of the human race. The Father punished the sinless One for the sinful ones; the innocent suffered for the guilty. Jesus Christ's suffering was beyond our comprehension.

You and I, on the other hand, have it far better than we think. True, we have problems and wrestle with temptations (Heb. 12:4), but it is not as bad as we often think. Even though "nothing is more natural for a person than to overestimate the severity of his trials,"[73] so far, we have not shed any blood resisting sin. Therefore, do not grow weary; do not lose heart (v. 3).

Responses to Chastening

So, what is the problem? Why are we discouraged when we could be filled with faith? The writer of Hebrews answers, *"You have **forgotten** the exhortation which speaks to you as to sons"* (v. 5, emphasis mine). And what is the forgotten exhortation? Quoting Proverbs 3:11-12, he says:

---

[72] [1]Therefore we also, since we are surrounded by so great a cloud of witnesses, let us lay aside every weight, and the sin which so easily ensnares *us,* and let us run with endurance the race that is set before us, [2]looking unto Jesus, the author and finisher of *our* faith, who for the joy that was set before Him endured the cross, despising the shame, and has sat down at the right hand of the throne of God.

[3]For consider Him who endured such hostility from sinners against Himself, lest you become weary and discouraged in your souls. [4]You have not yet resisted to bloodshed, striving against sin. [5]And you have forgotten the exhortation which speaks to you as to sons . . . (Heb. 12:1-5).

[73]Zane C. Hodges, "Hebrews" in *The Bible Knowledge Commentary: An Exposition of the Scriptures,* vol. 2, John F. Walvoord and Roy B. Zuck, eds. (Wheaton: Victor Books, 1985), 810.

112

*"My son, do not **despise** the chastening of the Lord,*
*Nor be **discouraged** when you are rebuked by Him;*
For whom the Lord loves He chastens,
And scourges every son whom He receives" (Heb. 12:5-6, emphasis mine).

He continued.

[7]*If you **endure** chastening, God deals with you as with sons; for what son is there whom a father does not chasten? [8]But if you are without chastening, of which all have become partakers, then you are illegitimate and not sons. [9]Furthermore, we have had human fathers who corrected **us**, and we paid **them respect**. Shall we not much more readily be in **subjection** to the Father of spirits and live? [10]For they indeed for a few days chastened **us** as seemed **best** to them, but He for **our** profit, that **we** may be partakers of His holiness. [11]Now no chastening seems to be joyful for the present, but painful; nevertheless, afterward it yields the peaceable fruit of righteousness to those who have been **trained** by it.*

In previous chapters we defined chastening, noted its benefits, and described and illustrated four levels of chastening. Now we conclude with the responses God's children make when they are chastened.

According to Hebrews 12, we can respond to the Father's chastening (discipline, child training, education/instruction) in at least six ways. Three of the responses are negative and three are positive.

Negative Responses

Three negative responses are in verse 5. We can forget, despise, and be discouraged by chastening. These responses do not please our Father for obvious reasons.

Forget

We can forget His chastening. "You have forgotten the exhortation which speaks to you as to sons." "Forgotten" is the translation of the Greek word meaning "to forget completely."[74] The believer is indifferent. Other priorities are on his mind. He is facing life's challenges without considering God's chastening. God's purpose is not on his radar.

---

[74]Spiros Zodhiates, *The Complete Word Study Dictionary: New Testament* (Chattanooga, TN: AMG Publishers, 2000), s.v., "ἐκλανθάνω; *eklanthánō*."

As a result, the believer's heart becomes insensitive and unresponsive. He or she despises the Lord's chastening, which is the second negative response.

Despise

"My son, do not despise the chastening of the LORD." This is an imperative, a command.

"Despise" means to "care little for, to consider of small worth."[75] Imagine a Christian saying, "God is talking, but it doesn't matter to me. It isn't significant, so I'm not listening." As shocking as it may sound, that is exactly what we do when we forget and despise our Father's chastening.

Discouraged

On the other hand, we can be discouraged when He rebukes. *"Nor be discouraged when you are rebuked by Him."* This too is a command.

"Discouraged" means to be weary, exhausted, or faint.[76] The word was used to describe an unstrung bow.[77] The string hangs limply, and the bow is unable to fulfill its purpose. It cannot shoot an arrow. That is a vivid picture of one who is discouraged by chastening. He or she has given up in despair. Emotionally, he has assumed the fetal position under his desk.

The three negative, fruitless responses are not the Father's plan. They are not the way He intends for us to respond to His chastening, and they will not lead to the benefits of chastening.

Positive Responses

Instead, we can endure, submit to, and be trained by chastening. These are positive responses.

Endure

"If you endure chastening, God deals with you as with sons; for what son is there whom a father does not chasten?" When we endure chastening we persevere; we do not quit. Literally, the word means to remain under a load.[78] Our Lord Jesus set the example for us. He *"endured the cross"* (v. 2) and *"endured . . . hostility from sinners"* (v. 3). We are

---

[75]Ibid., s.v., "ὀλιγωρέω; *oligōréō*."

[76]Ibid., s.v., "ἐκλύω; *eklúō*."

[77]H. G. Liddell, *A Lexicon: Abridged from Liddell and Scott's Greek-English Lexicon* (Oak Harbor, WA: Logos Research Systems, Inc., 1996), s.v., "ἐκ-λύω."

[78]Zodhiates, s.v., "ὑπομένω; *hupoménō*."

glad Jesus did not quit when He faced the cross. He fulfilled His greater purpose, and so can we.

Chastening is not child-abuse. It is God's loving action toward His children. It is the father working in us and training us to fulfill His greater purpose in our lives. "Discipline is an essential element in a father-son relationship: as in human families, so also within the family of God."[79] Chastening indicates the Father is as deeply involved in our lives as He was in the Lord Jesus' earthly life.

Submit

Further, if we submit to chastening, we place ourselves under His authority. "*We have had human fathers who corrected **us**, and we paid **them** respect. Shall we not much more readily be in subjection to the Father of spirits and live?*" (v. 9, emphasis mine). "Subjection" is the translation of a military term, meaning to rank under the authority of another. It assumes one is obeying orders.[80] Also, notice the motivation for our submission. Just as we respected and submitted to our human fathers' correction, we submit to the heavenly Father's chastening because we respect Him. Our response to chastening is a relationship and attitude issue.

Trained

Finally, we can be trained by chastening. "*Now no chastening seems to be joyful for the present, but painful; nevertheless, afterward it yields the peaceable fruit of righteousness to those who have been trained by it*" (v. 11). The Greek word, translated "trained," literally means to train naked, as did the Greek athletes, or simply, to exercise. It also gives us the English word gymnasium, a place to exercise.[81] This definition is initially a surprise. What does "training naked" have to do with our response to chastening? The answer is in Hebrews 4:12-13.

> [12]*For the word of God is living and powerful, and sharper than any two-edged sword, piercing even to the division of soul and spirit, and of joints and marrow, and is a discerner of the thoughts and*

---

[79]Paul Ellingworth, *The Epistle to the Hebrews*, in *New International Greek Testament Commentary* (Grand Rapids: Eerdmans, 1993), 649, as quoted in David L. Allen, *Hebrews* in *The New American Commentary*, vol. 35 (Nashville: B & H Publishing Group, 2010), 580.

[80]Zodhiates, s.v., "ὑποτάσσω; *hupotássō*."

[81]Ibid., s.v., γυμνάζω; *gumnázō*.

intents of the heart. [13]And there is no creature hidden from His sight, but all things are naked and open to the eyes of Him to whom we must give account.

The penetrating power of God's living and active Word is sharper than any double-edged sword. It reaches our innermost being. It critiques our thoughts and attitudes. Nothing can be hidden from God. He knows what we do, what we intend to do, and why. Everything is naked and open to His eyes, and it is to Him we will ultimately answer.

Therefore, to be "trained" by chastening, in part, means to learn to be totally open and honest with God. This training is connected to our devotional lives. When we read and meditate on His Word we become sensitive and responsive to what our Bible says. Like an athlete whose repetitive training has honed automatic reflexes, we can be trained to automatically respond to God's Word. The trained response is a fruit of the Father's child training through His Word.

Our Choice

We have choices. We choose our responses. What choices are you making? How are you responding to the heavenly Father's chastening in your life?

Do not forget, despise, or be discouraged. Rather, endure, submit, and be trained.

How can we be sure to make the positive rather than the negative responses? I believe the answer is in understanding the six responses as a chiasm.[82] The first and last responses go together, as do the second and fifth, and the third and fourth. The first response is negative and its corresponding response is positive. We can make the second response rather than the first. Instead of (A) forgetting the Father's chastening, we

---

[82]A chiasm or *chiastic structuring* is a literary device used by Old and New Testament writers. They use it to build up to their *main point* and then back off from it in the reverse order. For example:

A
  B
    C The main point the writer is making
    C^1 often lies at the center.
  B^1
A^1

A and A^1 may help to explain each other, as may B and B^1, C and C^1. Commentators note multiple chiasms in the book of Hebrews.

can be (A^1) trained by it. Rather than (B) despising His chastening, we can (B^1) submit because we respect Him. Rather than (C) being discouraged, we can (C^1) endure. With these contrasts, we will conclude our study.

Chapter 15

FORGET *OR* BE TRAINED

First, we can avoid forgetting the Father's chastening. Instead, we can be trained by His chastening.

God created us with perfect memories. Forgetting is a result of our fallen natures.[83] I regularly demonstrated my participation in the fall when I was around eight years old. I was forgetful. I did not think my forgetfulness was a problem, but Dad disagreed. He wanted to help me far more than I wanted help.

The Problem: Forgetting

Mom always had supper on the table, hot and ready to serve, at 5:30 PM. When Dad sat down for family Bible reading and prayer before the meal, he expected all of his children to be present.

"Don't forget," Dad would say, "supper will be at 5:30. Be here, ready to eat. What time Truman?"

"I know, Dad. 5:30."

I loved sports. I loved playing outdoors with my friends. We had so much fun I often forgot about the time. I did not have a watch, but it did not matter. I would have forgotten to check the time.

---

[83]William Gouge, *Commentary on Hebrews* (Grand Rapids: Kregel Publications, 1980; reprint of 1866 ed.), 939.

118

When our game paused and I realized I was getting hungry, reality hit. "O no," I said, "I forgot! I've got to go home." I ran home knowing I was late, but hoping I was not. Several times I ran into the house to find supper over, the food put away, and the dishes washed. My dad was waiting, belt in-hand, and I knew I was in trouble.

I tried to help my dad understand the problem. "Dad," I said, "I'm sorry. I just forgot." As far as I was concerned, that was an irrefutable defense. Had we been in court, I was sure an impartial Judge would say, "Not guilty. Case closed. Go enjoy your supper."

I did not forget on purpose. I did not want to be late. I did not want to miss supper. I wanted to be on time, and I certainly wanted to eat. I was hungry. I just forgot. Surely it is not fair to discipline someone who forgot by accident. At least, that is what I thought.

Dad listened but was unconvinced. "I understand, son," he said, "and I have something to help you remember."

Dad believed men should remember and fulfill their responsibilities. He was convinced that responsible men are faithful husbands and fathers, conscientious church members and citizens, and dependable business owners and employees. Responsible men are the future of the family, the church, and the nation.

Dad also believed that responsible boys become responsible men. He embraced his duty to help his son become a responsible man.

When I repeatedly missed supper, I forgot my father's exhortation. Dad believed discipline would help me remember. He believed it would help me become a responsible man.

I was a slow learner but Dad did not give up. He disciplined me until I was trained to remember his exhortation. And the training process was often painful (compare Heb. 12:11).

My forgetfulness is an example of a universal problem among Christians. The Bible exhorts us to remember, meditate on, and repeat truth—so that we will not forget. Our forgetfulness, however, is a heart problem, not a memory problem.

The Bible says, *"And you have forgotten the exhortation which speaks to you as to sons"* (Heb. 12:5). An exhortation is an "admonition or encouragement for the purpose of strengthening and establishing the believer in the faith."[84] God speaks to His sons and daughters through His Word. He speaks to us to build our faith. His exhortations are both correction and encouragement.

The writer of Hebrews noted, "God spoke to you like a father to his child, but you forgot what He said." When you think about it, it is

---

[84]Zodhiates, s.v., "παράκλησις; *paráklēsis*."

astonishing. We would never forget a personal communication from the President or Prime Minister of our country. How can we forget an exhortation from the Almighty? Yet we do. The verb translated "forgotten" (v. 5) emphasizes that we can completely forget His exhortation.[85] If we do, it is a heart problem, not a memory problem.

When we forget our Father's exhortations about the significance of our chastening, but remember other things, we reveal our true priorities.

You and I think about the things that are important to us—not what we aspire to think is important, but what we actually think is important. We do not forget priorities. When I said, "But Dad, I just forgot," he knew suppertime was not my priority. Playing was. That occupied my thoughts. That was most important to me.

The Remedy: Be Trained

Dad disciplined me to change my priorities, and it ultimately worked. Because of Dad's repeated, consistent discipline, I developed an internal alarm that went off when 5:30 approached. No matter where I was, what game I was playing, or how much fun I was having, when suppertime neared, I would suddenly think, "It must be nearly 5:30. I've got to go home." As a result, I never missed supper again.[86]

Dad's discipline moved me from my agenda to his agenda. And so it is with the heavenly Father's chastening.

What is the answer to a forgetful heart? We can be trained by chastening. "*Now no chastening seems to be joyful for the present, but painful; nevertheless, afterward it yields the peaceable fruit of righteousness to those who have been trained by it*" (v. 11). Chastening is often unpleasant, but it is good for us. If the Father's chastening has trained us, our hearts are naked and open to Him. We do not try to hide things from Him. We open the Word and automatically tune in to His voice. Like fine-tuned athletes, we have an obedience-response to His Word.

Athletes train by repeating their techniques over and over thousands of times. They develop what is called "muscle memory." A

---

[85]The word "is intensified in Greek by the prepositional prefix as well as being in the perfect tense, implying the notion of 'completely.'" Allen, 579.

[86]My dad died many years ago. I will see him in heaven one day because he trusted Jesus Christ as his Savior. I hope to thank him again for not being too lazy or unloving to train me for manhood. I often remember my dad's words and smile. Sometimes I laugh when I remember him saying, "I know you don't mean to forget, but this will help you remember." He was right and I am thankful to God.

professional basketball player, for example, spends thousands of hours in the gymnasium, repeating moves and shots hundreds of thousands of times. Muscle memory makes their moves automatic. They react without thinking. Their split-second responses make them one in a million. Likewise, those who are trained by the Father's chastening can immediately respond to the Holy Spirit's promptings. They have been trained daily in the gymnasium of God's Word.

> *"For everyone who partakes only of milk **is unskilled** in the word of righteousness, for he is a babe. But solid food belongs to those who are of full age, **that is**, those who **by reason of use have their senses exercised** to discern both good and evil"* (Heb. 5:13-14, emphasis mine).

Those whose hearts are "trained" are not forgetful hearers, but are doers of the Word. As James said:

> *22But be **doers** of the word, and not **hearers** only, deceiving yourselves. 23For if anyone is a **hearer** of the word and not a **doer**, he is like a man observing his natural face in a mirror; 24for he observes himself, goes away, and immediately forgets what kind of man he was. 25But he who looks into the perfect law of liberty and continues **in it**, and is not a **forgetful hearer** but a **doer** of the word, this one will be blessed in what he does* (James 1:22-25, emphasis mine).

The blessing comes from doing the Word, not just hearing it. Are you a forgetful hearer or a trained hearer? Are you daily opening the Word and allowing the Father to move you from your agenda to His agenda? Are you allowing Him to train you to have a responsive heart?

Chapter 16

DESPISE *OR* SUBMIT

The Problem: Despising

Second, we can either despise chastening or submit to chastening. God said, *"My son, do not despise the chastening of the Lord"* (v. 5). Remember that despise means to think little of His chastening, to treat it as an insignificant thing. King Asa's example warns us that God's children can have responsive hearts for many years, yet if we begin to drift spiritually, we may despise the Lord's chastening.

The Answer: Submit

The answer to this negative response is to submit to the Father because we respect Him. *"Furthermore, we have had human fathers who corrected **us**, and we paid **them** respect. Shall we not much more readily be in subjection to the Father of spirits and live"* (v. 9, emphasis mine).

We should have complete respect for our heavenly Father. He is spirit and He is perfect (Matt. 5:48). Earthly fathers, in contrast, have moral failures. They are imperfect; they are human. Even the best parents fall short in their correction and child training. Our heavenly Father does not. He chastens us according to His perfect wisdom, love, and purpose.[87]

---

[87]I believe Hebrews 12:9 assumes that fathers who correct their children will be in submission to God who corrects them. I have counseled many people whose view of

When we submit to the Father, we respect His rank and authority. We pledge our loyalty and obedience to Him. We no longer treat His chastening as if it were insignificant.

Remember, the Greek word, translated "submit," means to arrange under, to subordinate, to obey, to submit to one's control, yielding to one's admonition or advice. It was used as a military term meaning, "to arrange [troop divisions] in a military fashion under the command of a leader." In non-military use, it was "a voluntary attitude of giving in, cooperating, assuming responsibility, and carrying a burden"[88]

In the military a Sergeant gives orders to a lower ranking Private. "Private, make your bunk, scrub the latrine, fall down and do 100 push-ups." The Private obeys the Sergeant because of his position and rank. In many cases, the Private obeys outwardly but chafes inwardly. His attitude is not at all submissive to the one in authority over him. The Sergeant is indifferent to the Private's attitude; his concern is immediate, unquestioned obedience.

The secular view of submission often leads to abuse. It is often exercised from a position of power and authority over another. Priority is given to the self-interest of the one in authority.

Biblical submission is different. It exercises power and authority for the good of the one who is in submission. Authority and power are used to give servant leadership, not dictatorship. The ultimate model of servant leadership is the Lord Jesus, our good shepherd. His leadership is exercised out of love for those who submit to Him.

Authority Without Submission:
King Rehoboam

Consider the example of Solomon's son, King Rehoboam. He rejected his grandfather's view of authority and submission. David, his grandfather, was a Shepherd King, Servant King. Rehoboam embraced his father's example, given during the years when Solomon was not

---

God the Father was distorted by their dad's poor, and sometimes abusive, parenting. They unconsciously assume that God is like their dad. An abusive father will almost certainly influence his children to impute similar moral imperfections to God. This may be one reason that chastening is such a difficult subject for young Christians in this generation. Those who hear that God is a heavenly Father, and desire to seek Him because they have such respect for their earthly fathers, are truly blessed. Such fathers willingly submit themselves to God before they exercised authority over their children. If your view of God is distorted by faulty parenting, ask God's forgiveness. Look to the God of the Bible; do not create a false god in your own image or in your dad's image.

[88]James Strong, *Enhanced Strong's Lexicon* (Bellingham, WA: Logos Bible Software, 2001), s.v., "*hupotássō*; submit."

submissive to God. During those years the un-submissive king abused his subjects.

When Solomon's heart was responsive to God, he was in submission to God and His Word. He was a servant-leader like his father David. However, when his heart was hardened by sin, he became a dictator and abused his God-given position, power, and people.

After Solomon's death, his subjects pleaded with the newly crowned King Rehoboam. *"Your father made our yoke heavy,"* they said. *"Now therefore, lighten the burdensome service of your father, and his heavy yoke which he put on us, and we will serve you"* (1 Kings 12:4).

Rehoboam rejected the good advice of the older counselors. *"They spoke to him, saying, 'If you will be a servant to these people today, and serve them, and answer them, and speak good words to them, then they will be your servants forever'"* (v. 7). Some of the elders may have remembered King David's leadership. If so, they saw the contrast between David and Solomon's reigns. In effect they said, "If you will love and serve your people, they will love and serve you. They will respect you and be loyal to you because of mutual love, not because of your power-position over them."

Rehoboam fulfilled the old saying, "Like father, like son." His leadership was modeled after his father's poor example. *"Then the king answered the people roughly, and rejected the advice which the elders had given him; and he spoke to them according to the advice of the young men, saying, 'My father made your yoke heavy, but I will add to your yoke; my father chastised you with whips, but I will chastise you with scourges!'"* (vv. 13-14). Let me paraphrase: "I am the King; you are the servants. You will submit whether you like it or not. If you think my father was harsh, you haven't seen anything yet."

Leaders

The Bible contains many examples of leaders abusing their authority. They did not submit to God's authority, and the end result was conflict; people resisted their leadership.

Husbands

Many husbands abuse their authority. They demand that their wives submit to them even though they refuse to submit to God. They forget the exhortation, *"Christ is head of the church; . . . Husbands, love your wives, just as Christ also loved the church and gave Himself for*

124

her, . . . So husbands ought to love their own wives as their own bodies" (Eph. 5:23, 25, 28). Jesus Christ is the model for husbands. Sacrificial love is the hallmark of His headship. A wife will happily follow her husband when he demonstrates Christ-like headship. In contrast, she will resist her husband's headship if he is like Solomon and Rehoboam. She knows when he demands submission from her but is not submissive to God.

Parents

Many parents abuse their parental authority for the same reason. Parents demand respect and submission from their children when they do not respect and submit to God's authority over them. Children despise hypocritical child training; they do not respect and submit.

My Un-Submissive Attitude

Parents have authority over their children. The authority is God-given. Children are to obey their parents. However, it is not a burden too heavy to bear. In fact, the fifth commandment (Ex. 20:12) is the first commandment with an added promise: *"that your days may be long on the earth"* (Eph. 6:3). Obedience brings blessings.

While some parents are unworthy of the respect due them, my mother was worthy. She walked with God. When she prayed, God answered. I feared my mother's prayers more than I feared my daddy's belt. I experienced the belt many times, but I knew that God spoke through my mother.

Mother did not lord it over me; she used her position and authority for my good. She exercised her authority with wisdom and love because she was under her heavenly Father's authority.

One day, in the spring of my first grade year, it was a beautiful, warm day, and I wanted to go barefooted. I said, "Mom can I go barefooted after school?"

She said, "No indeed. You've got to wear your shoes. If you take your shoes off, you will probably step on a broken Coke bottle and cut your foot wide open."

Her answer did not satisfy me; it was not the one I wanted. At first I argued with her, but then I thought, "I'll tell her what she wants to hear, then I'll do what I want to do. She'll never know."

"OK, Mother," I conceded, "I won't take my shoes off after school. I'll wear my shoes when I walk home."

I did not think my mother knew what she was talking about. "I am careful," I thought. "I can see where I am walking; I know what I'm doing." So after school I took my shoes off to walk home barefooted. I planned to put them back on before I got close enough to the house for my mother to see me.

When I stepped into the grass it felt good on my feet. Being barefooted made me happy, but I remembered my mother's final words that morning. "If you take your shoes off, you will probably step on a broken Coke bottle and cut your foot wide open."

I walked a few feet, and I was extra careful. I watched where I was walking. I looked before taking each step, and I can now say my mother's warning did not come true, technically. I did not step on a broken Coca-Cola bottle.[89] It was a broken RC bottle, hidden by a clump of grass. I did not see it, but I certainly felt it cut into my foot. I could not walk.

A man saw me sitting on the ground bleeding and crying. He brought a towel to wrap my foot, picked me up, and carried me home. By the time we reached my house, his towel was soaked with my blood.

The moment I stepped on the broken bottle, I was thinking about my mother's warning. God also reminded me of my mother's authority over me. He seemed to say, "Your mother is lined up under My authority. When you disobey her, you are disobeying Me." That day, I learned a little more about fearing God and respecting my mother's authority.

The cut left a permanent scar on my foot, and a perpetual reminder in my heart. Since then, every time I put on my socks and shoes, I am reminded that I am under authority. And the reminder has adjusted my attitude. The scar is a mark of ownership that reminds me to submit to, rather than despise, God's child training.

I must admit, however, that I was a slow learner. In fact, the learning process continues. I am still learning submission. Apparently, it is a life-long project.

When I was 12 years old, my dad gave me the weekly responsibility of mowing the lawn. He also gave me specific instructions. He wanted the freshly mown lawn to have a particular, visible pattern. After a few weeks, I decided I knew a better way than my dad's way. So, along with Frank Sinatra and Elvis, "I did it my way." I soon discovered, however, that neither Frank nor Elvis had to answer to my dad. I had no choice but to do it his way.

---

[89]Actually, in our vernacular, every soft drink was a "Coke," no matter the brand.

Soon I was mowing the lawn each week, exactly the way Dad demanded, but I had a grumpy attitude. I was out of fellowship with Dad and I missed out on the joy of serving him. Rather than my work giving a sense of accomplishment, my attitude made the weekly mowing a traumatic experience.

Going barefooted and mowing the lawn may not seem like spiritual challenges, but they were for me. I had to learn to submit to rather than despise my parents' instructions. God used my parents to fine-tune my heart and teach me the art of joyfully submitting to my heavenly Father.

Jesus, Our Example of Submission

Our Lord Jesus, of course, did not have a problem submitting to His heavenly Father or to His earthly parents. He is the perfect example of submitting to child training and instruction. *"Though He was a Son, **yet** He learned obedience by the things which He suffered"* (Heb. 5:8, emphasis mine). This does not mean Jesus had a tendency toward disobedience. It means His suffering perfectly fitted Him to obey the Father's will. He became our faithful High Priest; He understands all of our pains and needs. We are told, therefore, to *"look unto Jesus"* (Heb. 12:2) and *"consider Him"* (v. 3).

Jesus is fully God. He is co-equal and co-eternal with God the Father and God the Holy Spirit. Yet, when He came to earth, He humbled Himself, became a man, and submitted to the Father's will. His humility is described in Philippians 2.

> *[5]Let this mind be in you which was also in Christ Jesus, [6]who, being in the form of God, did not consider it robbery to be equal with God, [7]but made Himself of no reputation, taking the form of a bondservant, **and** coming in the likeness of men. [8]And being found in appearance as a man, He humbled Himself and became obedient to **the point of** death, even the death of the cross. [9]Therefore God also has highly exalted Him and given Him the name which is above every name, [10]that at the name of Jesus every knee should bow, of those in heaven, and of those on earth, and of those under the earth, [11]and **that** every tongue should confess that Jesus Christ is Lord, to the glory of God the Father* (Phil. 2:5-11).

Jesus had all authority and power in heaven and earth. He could have done what Rehoboam planned to do to Israel. He could have forced everyone's obedience. Instead, Jesus took on the form of a bondservant. He modeled the kind of submission He commended to His disciples, the submission that makes one great.

> *[25]But Jesus called them to **Himself** and said, "You know that the rulers of the Gentiles **lord it over them**, and those who are great exercise authority over them. [26]Yet it shall not be so among you; but whoever desires to become great among you, let him be your **servant**. [27]And whoever desires to be first among you, let him be your slave— [28]just as the Son of Man did not come to be served, but **to serve**, and **to give** His life a ransom for many"* (Matt. 20:25-28, emphasis mine).

Jesus is Lord, but He did not "Lord it over" people. He had a servant's heart. He willingly gave His life to serve and save others. Biblical submission is revealed by a servant's heart and a servant's attitude. Those who are submissive to God are willing to humble themselves to be concerned for others. *"**Let** nothing **be done** through strife or vainglory; but in lowliness of mind let each esteem others better than themselves. Look not every man on his own things, but every man also on the things of others"* (Phil. 2:3-4, emphasis).

Jesus Submitted to Joseph and Mary

Jesus' submissive heart was first revealed when He was twelve years old. Because He first submitted to His heavenly Father, Jesus willingly submitted to Joseph and Mary. *"Then He went down with them and came to Nazareth, and was subject to them"* (Luke 2:51).

The context is important. Joseph, Mary, and Jesus traveled to Jerusalem for the annual Passover. Afterward, the residents of Nazareth returned home in a group. Jesus did not walk with Mary and Joseph during the first day, but they assumed he was walking with relatives or friends. When they camped for the evening, Jesus did not come to their campsite. They looked for Him, but He was not with their traveling companions. Naturally they were alarmed and rushed back to Jerusalem. After three days of frantic searching in the city, Mary and Joseph finally found Jesus in the temple, *"sitting in the midst of the teachers, both listening to them and asking them questions"* (Luke 2:46).

> *"So when they saw Him, they were amazed; and His mother said to Him, "Son, why have You done this to us? Look, Your father and I have sought You anxiously." And He said to them, "Why did you*

seek Me? Did you not know that I must be about My Father's business?" (vv. 48-49).

Jesus' question was not whiny, arrogant, or rebellious. It was an honest question. His parents knew who He was. What else did they expect Him to be doing? But notice, He went home with them and submitted to them (v. 51).

The rotation of the earth, the movements of the solar system, and all the tiny atoms in the universe were subject to Jesus (Col. 1:17), yet He submitted to Joseph and Mary. The earth's weather, the birds of the air, and the beasts of the fields, were all subject to Jesus, yet He willingly submitted to Joseph. He was smarter than Joseph, yet he submitted. He was perfect and pure, yet he submitted to an imperfect and sinful father. Consider the One who voluntarily made Himself subject to Joseph and Mary.

[15]He is the image of the invisible God, the firstborn over all creation. [16]For everything was created by Him, in heaven and on earth, the visible and the invisible, whether thrones or dominions or rulers or authorities—all things have been created through Him and for Him. [17]He is before all things, and by Him all things hold together. [18]He is also the head of the body, the church; He is the beginning, the firstborn from the dead, so that He might come to have first place in everything.
[19]For God was pleased to have all His fullness dwell in Him, and through Him to reconcile everything to Himself by making peace through the blood of His cross whether things on earth or things in heaven (Col. 1:15-20).

The One who created the world submitted to human parents. Why did He submit to them when He was smarter, more powerful, and superior to them in every way? The fifth of the Ten Commandments declares, *"Honor your father and your mother"* (Ex. 20:12), and He perfectly obeyed God's law. He saw their imperfections in contrast to His perfection. Yet, He humbled Himself and submitted Himself to His earthly parents. He obeyed His parents; He honored their God-given authoritative position over Him.

Joseph was a carpenter. Jesus worked with him and learned the trade from him. But think about it. Can you imagine Joseph teaching Jesus how to build furniture when Jesus had built the universe? This is a form of submission that we know nothing about. Jesus was wiser than His stepfather, but He submitted. He could have introduced better methods and tools for carpentry, but He kept a joyful, submissive attitude as He worked for and with Joseph. He restrained Himself. He did not exercise His power to miraculously create furniture. He could have, of course. A few years later, He proved His authority over nature when He multiplied loaves and fish to feed 5,000, walked on water, and calmed a raging storm with a single command.

Jesus' ministry to Israel began when John the Baptist baptized Him in the Jordan River and the Holy Spirit descended upon Him in the form of a dove. He was fully God, full of the Holy Spirit, full of authority, and full of power. Even so, He did all His heavenly Father led Him to do, but only what His heavenly Father led Him to do. As Jesus had submitted to Joseph and Mary, so He submitted to His heavenly Father. Jesus did not act independently. He lined up under the Father's authority. He submitted with a perfect attitude of love and joy. He is our perfect model of submission.

At the end of Jesus' ministry on earth, Jesus presented Himself to the Father. He prayed in the Garden of Gethsemane. He faced the torture of the cross and the contradiction of Holiness being made sin. Still, He submitted to the Father for the sake of our salvation. He prayed, "*Not My will, but Yours, be done*" (Luke 22:42).

How can we submit? We can "look to Jesus" and "consider Him." He endured hostility from sinners and submitted to the Father's will. By the way, neither hostility nor submission stole His joy, and neither will steal our joy. Do not despise the Father's chastening; submit to His child training. Jesus Christ is our perfect example of submission (Heb. 12:2-3).

Chapter 17

ROYAL SUBMISSION

According to conventional wisdom, an ancient King was sovereign over his realm. The King submitted to no one; all of his subjects submitted to him. His word was law. His will was unquestioned. His commands were obeyed. Criticism of the king was a capital offense. On the spot decapitation was not an unusual sentence—no trial, no appeal, no mercy. Such was the practice of ancient superpowers such as Egypt, Assyria, Babylon, and Persia.[90]

Conventional wisdom did not apply to Israel's monarchy. Kings of Israel served at God's pleasure and under God's sovereign authority. God's Word was law in Israel; His will was to be obeyed without question. Israel's king was to remember that he too was a man in need of forgiveness and grace. Therefore, he was to balance law with grace and mercy as he ruled and related to God's people. Of all the kings of Israel, none understood this fact more clearly than David.

We have noted that David's grandson, Rehoboam, misunderstood the purpose and plan for Israel's monarchy. He thought he had the right to "chastise" his subjects "with scourges" to force their submission to him (1 Kings 12:11). He did not understand that the Father's intention was to chasten him. The Father wanted to train Rehoboam to be a wise, compassionate, Spirit-filled ruler of Israel. Instead, Rehoboam demanded submission without being submissive.

---

[90]For example, Daniel said of Nebuchadnezzar, King of Babylon, "All peoples, nations, and languages trembled and feared before him. Whomever he wished, he executed; whomever he wished, he kept alive" (Dan. 5:19).

David, however, recognized the uniqueness of Israel's monarchy. He realized that his reign was but a preparation for his Messianic descendant who would someday come to redeem sinners and reign over the whole world (2 Sam. 7:12, 16; 1 Chron. 17:10-12). We now know the coming redeemer is none other than Jesus Christ, the "Son of David" (Matt. 1:1) who came to *save His people from their sins"* (Matt. 1:21; Luke 1:31-35).

David understood his greater purpose and that chastening was the Father's process of training and equipping him. He knew he was responsible to co-operate with the training. The Scriptures record several examples of King David submitting to the Father's chastening. In this brief chapter, we will consider one unusual account.

No Conventional Wisdom

A weary, disheartened caravan of refugees trudged along a dusty road leading away from Jerusalem. David was at the center of the refugees. Fortunately for a man named Shimei, David's heart was tuned to the Father's heart; he did not bow to conventional wisdom. The story is a vivid example of David's insight into God's work in his life.

⁵When King David got to Bahurim, a man belonging to the family of the house of Saul was just coming out. His name was Shimei son of Gera, and he was yelling curses as he approached. [Remember, according to conventional wisdom, this was a capital crime. To make matters worse,] *⁶He threw stones at David and at all the royal servants, the people and the warriors on David's right and left. ⁷Shimei said as he cursed: "Get out, get out, you worthless murderer! ⁸The LORD has paid you back for all the blood of the house of Saul in whose place you became king, and the LORD has handed the kingdom over to your son Absalom. Look, you are in trouble because you're a murderer!"*

⁹Then Abishai son of Zeruiah said to the king, "Why should this dead dog curse my lord the king? Let me go over and cut his head off!" [It was the expected sentence. But notice David's answer.]

¹⁰The king replied, "Sons of Zeruiah, do we agree on anything? He curses me this way because the LORD told him, 'Curse David!' Therefore, who can say, 'Why did you do that?'" ¹¹Then David said to Abishai and all his servants, "Look, my own son, my own flesh *and blood, intends to take my life—how much more now this Benjaminite! Leave him alone and let him curse me; the LORD has told him to. ^{12}Perhaps the LORD will see my affliction and restore goodness to me instead of Shimei's curses today." ^{13}So David and his men proceeded along the road as Shimei was going along the ridge of the hill opposite him. As Shimei went, he cursed David, and threw stones and dirt at him. ^{14}Finally, the king and all the people with him arrived exhausted, so they rested there* (2 Sam. 16:5-14 HCSB).

David had the authority to send one of his loyal soldiers to cut off Shimei's head. Abishai (who, by the way, wanted to kill Saul in his sleep, 1 Samuel 26:8) volunteered to dispense with Shimei. He said, "Let me go over and cut his head off!" Abishai's advice was common sense. He had "observed that people without heads do not curse."[91]

David, however, had been humbled by the Father's chastening. It had yielded "the peaceable fruit of righteousness" in his life; he had "been trained by it" (Heb. 12:11). His heart was again responsive. It was in tune with the Father's heart and his eyes were on the Father's eyes, so he spared Shimei's life.

Shimei was a member of Saul's family (2 Sam. 16:5). Like Saul, he was a pawn in Satan's hand. His vicious cursing was unjustified. Even so, sometimes God uses the Devil as His messenger boy. David understood that God was using Shimei in his life, and he submitted to the chastening.

As David left Saul in God's hands, both in the cave and in the slumbering camp, so he left Shimei in God's hands. He did not avenge himself.

Wise Submission

If we are unaware of the context, this is a strange story to say the least. Why did David and his loyal followers flee Jerusalem? How did David know God was chastening him? The story, in its context, answers these questions. It reveals how David knew and submitted to the Father's discipline. It also points to helpful reminders as we submit to, rather than despise, our Father's child training.

Notice how you and I can submit to our Father's chastening?

---

[91]Davis, *2 Samuel*, 165.

Accept God's Word

First, accept God's Word. Do not argue with your Bible. It will always guide you to the truth about God and about yourself. Be willing to listen. Accept what God says, even if it is surprising or uncomfortable.

> [12]*For the word of God is living and powerful, and sharper than any two-edged sword, piercing even to the division of soul and spirit, and of joints and marrow, and is a discerner of the thoughts and intents of the heart. [13]And there is no creature hidden from His sight, but all things are naked and open to the eyes of Him to whom we must give account* (Heb. 4:12-13).

When Nathan the prophet confronted David with his sins against Bathsheba and Uriah, God's Word cut David to the heart. He did not argue, deny, or defend himself. David accepted God's Word. Nathan said:

> [11]*"Thus says the LORD: 'Behold, I will raise up adversity against you from your own house; and I will take your wives before your eyes and give* **them** *to your neighbor, and he shall lie with your wives in the sight of this sun. [12]For you did* **it** *secretly, but I will do this thing before all Israel, before the sun.'"*
> [13]*So David said to Nathan, "I have sinned against the LORD." And Nathan said to David, "The LORD also has put away your sin; you shall not die"* (2 Sam. 12:11-13, emphasis mine).

God was gracious. David repented and confessed his sins, and God forgave him. He will do the same for you and me.

If we confess our sins, the blood of Jesus Christ cleanses us from all sin (1 John 1:7, 9). Forgiveness is complete, total, and absolute. Fellowship with the Father is fully restored when we confess our sins.

On-Going Consequences

Some sins, however, have on-going consequences even after we are forgiven. A terrible disease contracted through a sinful lifestyle is an example. One will have the joy of forgiveness, but the disease may remain.

Forgiveness of sin and the on-going consequences of sin are not the same things. God forgave Adam and Eve for eating the forbidden fruit (Gen. 3:21), but they were still expelled from the Garden of Eden (vv. 22-24) and humanity was still plunged into sin (Rom. 5:12).

Some people, because of their positions, experience greater consequences for a sin than others experience. *"For everyone to whom much is given, from him much will be required"* (Luke 12:48). A Pastor or Bible teacher, for example, will "receive a stricter judgment" (James 3:1). And so it was with King David.

Because David was the nation's leader, he became "object lesson #1" that no one is above God's law. Sin has consequences no matter who you are. David had to endure public chastening for years.

David's Family Consequences

After David yielded to his lust for another man's wife, Satan seemed to have greater access to his family. One of the on-going, heartbreaking consequences of David's sin was an adversary among his own sons (2 Sam. 12:11). The adversary was Absalom, the firstborn of his wife *"Maacah, the daughter of Talmai, king of Geshur"* (2 Sam. 3:3). David was not innocent in Absalom's rebellion.

Amnon's Rape

David's son Amnon, by another wife, Ahinoam, lusted for his gorgeous half-sister Tamar (2 Sam. 13). Tamar was Absalom's full sister. Amnon's lust led to rape. David was angry when he heard about it. He fussed and fumed, but did nothing.

David's inaction planted seeds of disrespect and bitterness in Absalom's heart. Since Dad did nothing, Absalom took matters into his own hands. He took Tamar into his home and swore vengeance on Amnon. After about two years, he arranged Amnon's murder. Once the murder was carried out, Absalom fled to his mother's homeland for refuge.

Absalom's Coup

David allowed Absalom to return to Israel three years later. By then, Absalom's bitterness had grown into rebellion. He began a successful campaign of winning the hearts and the support of the people. When the time was right, he led a coup against his father. Surprisingly, most of Judah supported Absalom.

David's Responsive Heart

Absalom gathered an army and marched into Jerusalem. There was little resistance because David and his loyalist fled the city to lessen the bloodshed. During the flight from Absalom, Shimei attacked David with stones, dirt, and curses: "Get out, get out, you worthless murderer!"

David's responsive heart recognized what his soldiers did not. They saw and heard a wicked man, but David submitted to the Father's rod. He saw it as a part of the long-term consequences of his sin. Whereas David *"despised the commandment of the LORD"* (2 Sam. 12:9) when he committed adultery with Bathsheba, now he humbly submitted to the Father's rod, even though it was in the hand of a wicked man.

David accepted God's Word. He listened, learned, and submitted to God's discipline. You and I will be wise if we do the same.

Yield Your Rights

Second, yield your rights rather than demanding your rights. Christians are free from sins bondage, but we are not free to live any way we choose (Gal. 5:1).[92] We are free to submit our lives to Jesus Christ's Lordship. We are free to live Spirit-filled, victorious lives. We are free to die to our old life of sin and have the resurrected Lord Jesus live His life through us via the person and power of the indwelling Holy Spirit (Rom. 6:1-2, 11-14). The Bible says, *"Or do you not know that your body is the temple of the Holy Spirit **who is** in you, whom you have from God, and you are not your own? For you were bought with a price; therefore glorify God in your body and in your spirit, which are God's"* (1 Cor. 6:19-20).

Do you realize that God lives in you? As a result, you do not own yourself. Jesus paid the price to purchase you. He died in your place. You belong to Him. So, submit to God; glorify Him with your body. Surrender your rights to Him.

David yielded his rights. He yielded his right to be treated with *respect*. Shimei cursed him and threw stones and dirt at him (2 Sam. 16:5-6, 13). David yielded his right to immediately *execute* Shimei (vv. 9-10). He yielded his right to *defend himself against false accusations*. Shimei accused David in one area that he was blameless.

"The LORD has paid you back," said Shimei, *"for all the blood of the house of Saul"* (v. 8). David could have defended himself. He could

---

[92]Stand fast therefore in the liberty by which Christ has made us free, and do not be entangled again with a yoke of bondage (Gal. 5:1).

have reminded Shimei and his loyal supporters of how he spared Saul's life many times. He left Saul in God's hands when he could have shed Saul's blood. That weary day, David could have called many eyewitnesses to confirm his righteousness toward Saul and his house.

David knew that God had taken Saul's life in His time and His way. David could have screamed back, "I'm not guilty of Saul's blood." Shimei was wrong and David was right. Case closed. But submitting to God is not always about being right; it is about being responsive and humble before God.

David knew a secret that Shimei and his men did not know. Though not guilty of Saul's blood, David was guilty of faithful Uriah's blood. David deserved death for his sin against Bathsheba's husband, yet God forgave him.

We can learn a great lesson on humility and grace from David's response to Shimei. If we are accused of something of which we are not guilty, we know we were guilty of other sins, even though they are now long forgiven. A self-righteous defense and a submissive heart are incompatible. Like David, our hearts should be humbled in deep gratitude to God for His eternal grace and tender mercies toward us.

Why did David yield his rights? He accepted God's Word and submitted to the Father's chastening, even when the Father's rod was in the hands of a wicked man. David willingly allowed God to work in his life. He wanted to receive all of the benefits from his child training.

God may use a Shimei in our lives as well. If we accept God's Word and yield our rights, we can submit to God rather than react to the person. We can trust God to work all things together for our good and His glory (Rom. 8:28). Sometimes the question is not who is right or wrong, but will we yield our rights to God for the sake of His will and training. David did, and we can too.

Humility Required

Yielding our rights requires humility. We humble ourselves before God and the people He uses in our chastening. Submission and humility are inseparable. We cannot have one without the other. Further, we cannot be submissive and humble before God if we are unwilling to humble ourselves to the people He uses in our lives. The Apostle Peter said,

> *"You younger people, submit yourselves to **your** elders. Yes, all of **you** be submissive to one another, and be clothed with humility, for*

'God resists the proud, but gives grace to the humble'" (1 Peter 5:5, emphasis mine).

Humility precedes exaltation. When God intends to promote one to an exalted position, He first humbles that person. God wants to use His children mightily without them becoming proud and taking credit for their own success in ministry, business, or government. He will not share His glory with you or me or anyone else. He said,

*"I **am** the LORD, that **is** My name; and My glory I will not give to another, nor My praise to carved images* (Isa. 42:8, emphasis mine). *"Therefore humble yourselves under the mighty hand of God, that He may exalt you in due time"* (1 Peter 5:6).

Humility like David's was rare among ancient monarchs. He humbled himself to God and to man. He submitted to the Father's rod in Shimei's hand. King David said to Abishai, *"Leave him alone and let him curse me; the LORD has told him to"* (2 Sam. 16:11). The end result was that God defeated the coup and restored David to Israel's throne.

Expect Misunderstanding

Do not be surprised when your submission to the Father is misunderstood. Most will interpret it as "doormat theology." Well meaning friends will say, "Don't let people walk all over you. Stand up for your rights." Your priority, however, is not being understood. Your priority is pleasing God.

David's men misunderstood him. David said to Abishai, *"Sons of Zeruiah, do we agree on anything? He curses me this way because the LORD told him, 'Curse David!'"* (2 Sam. 16:10). Apparently, Abishai's brother, Joab (1 Sam. 26:6) agreed with him, and Joab was the commander of David's army (2 Sam. 8:16). Notice David said, "Sons of Zeruiah," not "son." Most, if not all, of the loyalist with David seemed to agree with Abishai's solution as well, for David spoke *"to Abishai and all his servants"* (2 Sam. 16:11). Humility and misunderstanding often go hand in hand. They are by-products of yielding our rights.

David focused on submitting to the Father's chastening, not on satisfying his friends. We will be wise to do the same.

Trust God's Grace

Third, when we are chastened we can trust God's grace. Even if our chastening is a correction for past sins, we never know how God may demonstrate His grace. Submitting to and learning from His child training is wise. David said to his loyal followers, *"It may be that the LORD will look on my affliction, and that the LORD will repay me with good for his cursing this day"* (v. 12).

> Here . . . is the secret of David's peace. Not in having Shimei's head on a platter but in . . . a deep-seated confidence in a God of unguessable grace, who has a tendency to replace cursing with goodness! He assumes that Yahweh has this strangely wonderful way of looking upon guilt and yet returning blessing instead of a curse. He senses that though the mouth of God has declared his punishment (12:10-12), the eye of God may long to spare him from it.[93]

Notice, however, that while David trusted God's grace, he did not presume upon God's grace. He did not act as if God owed him. He said, "It may be" or "perhaps." For one who trusts in grace, it cannot be otherwise. The essence of grace is that it is God's unearned, undeserved favor.

Where did David get such a radical idea? David had a personal relationship with God; he knew God's character. Even though his enemies were vicious, His God was gracious, and David trusted His grace. He said:

> *"O God, the proud* [Saul, Nabal, Shimei, and Absalom, to name just a few] *have risen against me, and a mob of violent **men** have sought my life, and have not set You before them.* [Their hearts were against God's king because they did not seek God with all their hearts.] But [in contrast to the enemies] *You, O Lord, **are** a God full of compassion, and gracious, longsuffering and abundant in mercy and truth"* (Ps. 86:14-15, emphasis mine).

Likewise, you and I can trust God's grace, even though some have little hope that God would ever be gracious to them again. Do you know some Christians who,

---

[93]Davis, *2 Samuel*, 167.

believe they've made a royal curse-job of their lives, [because] . . . with open eyes, [they] have smashed God's commandments and defied his standards, and then suffered miserably for it? [They have genuinely repented and been forgiven] . . . yet they are sure God only regards them with grudging toleration, and sometimes they doubt the toleration. They are, they think, doomed to the junkyard of Christian existence.[94]

If you not only know someone like that, but you are someone like that, here is great news. You can trust David's God. He had grace on the chief of sinners (1 Tim. 1:15), and He will have grace on you. He is the God who reverses curses. In fact, *"Christ has redeemed us from the curse of the law, having become a curse for us (for it is written, 'Cursed is everyone who hangs on a tree')"* (Gal. 3:13).

Rest in the Lord

Finally, rest in the Lord. We do not want to be guilty of over-spiritualizing an event, but notice how David's encounter with Shimei ended. *"And as David and his men went along the road, Shimei went along the hillside opposite him and cursed as he went, threw stones at him and kicked up dust. Now the king and all the people who **were** with him became weary; so they refreshed themselves there"* (2 Sam. 16:13-14, emphasis mine). David demonstrated the reality of Psalm 23:5, *"You prepare a table before me in the presence of my enemies."*

You and I can have the same experience with our gracious God. We are invited to:

Rest in the LORD, and wait patiently for Him; do not fret [worry] *because . . . of the man who brings wicked schemes to pass. Cease from anger, and forsake wrath; do not fret—**it** only **causes** harm. For evildoers shall be cut off* [in God's way and in God's time]; *but* [in contrast] *those who wait on the LORD, they shall inherit the earth. . . . And shall delight themselves in the abundance of peace* (Ps. 37:7-9, 11b, emphasis mine).

Do you want to rest in the Lord, be free from worry and anger, and enjoy peace overflowing in your life? Then respond to Jesus' invitation:

---

[94]Ibid.

140

*"Come to Me, all **you** who labor and are heavy laden, and I will give you rest"* (Matt. 11:28).

Conclusion

David did not despise his chastening. Rather, he endured chastening. He accepted God's Word, yielded his rights, and trusted God's grace. As a result, he was able to rest in the Lord in spite of his enemies. You and I can do the same. We too can submit to the Father's chastening.[95]

---

[95]A few additional lessons on submission come to mind. We learn from David:
- One who has authority over you does not have to be perfect, or always right, before you submit. Look beyond the earthly authority. Submit to God, your ultimate authority. He controls all things.
- Our submission to the Father is an example to those who are under our authority. God gives fathers circumstances where their children see them submit to God and to others. Dad's submission is a life-lesson that submission is part of the Heavenly Fathers child training.
- David's submission was a foreshadowing of Christ's submission to the Father's will. As David did not open his mouth to Shimei's mocking and cursing, Jesus faced far greater mocking and cursing, yet "opened not his mouth" (Isa. 53:7; Matt. 26:62-63; 27:12, 14; John 19:9; Acts 8:32). It was in our Lord Jesus' power to destroy the mockers, but He submitted to the Father to become our Passover Lamb. Unlike David, however, Jesus was sinless.
- Unless our hearts are sensitive and responsive to our heavenly Father, we will despise His chastening. We will count it to be of little value in our lives. We will see our circumstances as mere accidents, and fail to ask if He is instructing, correcting, or seeking to prevent us from going in the wrong direction. A sensitive heart will be in the Word daily, discerning and submitting to God's will.

Chapter 18

DISCOURAGED *OR* ENDURE

The Problem—Discouraged

Third, chastening can discourage us, or we can endure chastening. Our heavenly Father does not want us to be discouraged. Hebrews 12 commanded, *"Nor be discouraged when you are rebuked by Him"* (v. 5). He does not want us to be spiritually weary, exhausted, and defeated. He does not want us to respond to his rebukes, saying, "I can't do anything right. Someone's always on my case. I give up." He does not intend for chastening to make us as emotionally defeated as an unstrung bow.

How do we avoid discouragement?

The Answer—Endure

The answer to discouragement is endurance. We can endure chastening. We can persevere. We can remain under the load, refusing to quit. *"If you endure chastening, God deals with you as with sons; for what son is there whom a father does not chasten? But if you are without chastening, of which all have become partakers, then you are illegitimate and not sons"* (vv. 7-8).

The Father's chastening is a reminder that you are His child. You are a member of the royal family. Just as my dad never disciplined any of the neighbor's children, only my sisters and me, so God trains His children and only His children. He does not train the Devil's children.

How does our heavenly Father relate to unsaved people? He convicts them of their sins and warns them to repent. He invites them to trust His Son as their Savior. He invites them to be born again into His family, but the unsaved are not in His family and do not receive child training. So, if you are chastened, rejoice and endure.

Endure by Faith

Endurance is the heart of Hebrews 12:1-11. Endurance is the central point of the chiasm and the dominant theme of the passage. Just before unveiling "Faith's Hall of Fame" (Hebrews 11), the writer of Hebrews stated, *"For you have need of endurance, so that after you have done the will of God, you may receive the promise"* (10:36). All of the people listed in Hebrews 11 did just that; they endured by faith.

Our Example—Jesus Christ

In Hebrews 12, the writer focused on our ultimate example of endurance—Jesus Christ. We are encouraged to *"run with endurance the race that is set before us, looking unto Jesus . . . who . . . endured the cross . . .* [and] *endured such hostility from sinners"* (vv. 1-3). The mocking, the scourge, the crown of thorns, and the cross did not discourage Him. He endured the cross and the hostility for the Father's glory and our good.

Jesus did not quit when He faced the cross. When He was arrested in the Garden of Gethsemane, He told Peter to put away his sword. Jesus did not need Peter's protection. He asked, *"Do you think that I cannot now pray to My Father, and He will provide Me with more than twelve legions of angels?"* (Matt. 26:53). But Jesus did not call the angels. He chose to endure the shame and the pain. He remained under the load. He did not quit. He submitted to the Father's will and fulfilled His life's purpose; He paid the penalty for all of our sins.

Jesus is our example. We look to Him. You and I are encouraged to endure chastening *"lest you become weary and discouraged in your souls"* (v. 3). When we endure, good things happen; our hearts are tuned to the Father's heart and He is pleased.

Jesus not only endured the cross, He also endured Israel's rejection. They refused to acknowledge Him as their promised Messiah.

Yet, because His eyes were always on His Father's eyes and His heart was always responsive to the Father's heart, He was never discouraged in His ministry or mission.

Isaiah foresaw Jesus' atoning suffering and sacrifice (Isaiah 53). He also foresaw that Jesus would never be discouraged in His ministry or overwhelmed by His mission. *"Behold! My Servant whom I uphold, My Elect One **in whom** My soul delights! I have put My Spirit upon Him; He will bring forth justice to the Gentiles. . . . He will not fail nor be discouraged, till He has established justice in the earth"* (Isaiah 42:1, 4, emphasis mine).

The Father delighted in the Son. The Son was not discouraged because pleasing the Father was His delight.

David's Discouragement

Often, however, we are more like King David than we are like our Savior. David was a man after God's own heart, but he battled discouragement. After being delivered from Saul many times, David took his eyes off of God's promises. He became discouraged and pouted, "Someday I will perish at Saul's hand, therefore I will flee to the land of the Philistines and Saul will no longer seek my life" (my paraphrase of 1 Sam. 27:1).

Notice his next move. *"Then David arose and went over with the six hundred men who **were** with him to Achish the son of Maoch, king of Gath. So David dwelt with Achish at Gath, he and his men, each man with his household, **and** David with his two wives, Ahinoam the Jezreelitess, and Abigail the Carmelitess, Nabal's widow"* (vv. 2-3, emphasis mine). Ironically, David sought security in Goliath's home region (1 Sam. 17:4).

David ran from his problems into a spiritually dark period in his life. He lived with Israel's enemies for a year and four months (v. 7). He was unequally yoked with unbelievers and became backslidden. David no longer needed daily deliverance from Saul, but he no longer depended on God daily.

It appeared David made a wise choice. *Physically* and *emotionally*, things were better for David and his followers when they lived among the Philistines. A huge stress was lifted from their shoulders because *"it was told Saul that David had fled to Gath; so he sought him no more"* (1 Sam. 27:4). Perhaps they got their first full night of sleep in many months.

Financially, things were better. The King of Gath gave David a city, Ziklag, and he and his men prospered by raiding nearby settlements of other raiders. He took "*away the sheep, the oxen, the donkeys, the camels, and the apparel*" (v. 9). I am sure most of his loyal followers felt their lives were better after David compromised his convictions and used good common sense.

Yet, *spiritually*, things were worse; the Father was not pleased. During this time period, David did not endure, he did not submit, and he was not trained by the Father's chastening. His flesh dominated his faith. His emotions ruled him and his flesh almost ruined him. Lies, deceit, and cruelty characterized him during this dark period (vv. 8-12).

The depth of his spiritual decline was revealed as the Philistines armies prepared to go to war against Israel. The Philistine troops marched in review before their kings. David and his men marched behind Achish's troops (1 Sam. 29:2).

That day, David faced a huge dilemma. God anointed him to be Israel's King. Was he now willing to fight against Israel? Would he be loyal to his benefactor, Achish, or would he return to the Lord and submit to God's greater purpose for his life?

How did David entangle himself in this dilemma? Hebrews 12 gives the answer. The pattern is universal for God's children. It was the same for David and it will be the same for you and me.

The Path to Discouragement

First, David *forgot* the purpose and value of the Father's chastening. Second, he *despised* his child training. He treated it as if it were insignificant. As a result, third, he became *discouraged*. He thought God was working against him instead of for him.

Of course, discouragement was not the Father's plan. He intended for David to *be trained* by his chastening. He gave repeated reminders of His greater purpose for David's life. He used both friends and enemies to confirm and reconfirm Samuel's original proclamation that God had appointed and anointed David as Israel's future king (1 Sam. 16:1, 13).

Earlier we have noted dramatic scenes from David's child training in the wilderness. After each recorded scene of chastening, someone reconfirmed God's plan for David's life.

Scene One—You Shall Surely be King

Saul and 3000 of his best troops searched for David. Saul intended to kill him. Saul entered a cave where David and his men were hiding.

David spared Saul's life.[96] He cut off the corner of Saul's robe when he easily could have cut off his head. When Saul discovered David's mercy, he said, "*And now I know indeed that you shall surely be king, and that the kingdom of Israel shall be established in your hand*" (1 Sam. 24:20).

Scene Two—Appointed Ruler Over Israel

The next confirmation came after Nabal insulted David, and David reacted in the flesh (1 Sam. 25).[97] He would have killed many innocent people if he had not heard and responded to God's rebuke through Abigail.

A part of Abigail's rebuke reconfirmed God's future plan for David. She reminded David why he should not avenge himself. She said:

"And it shall come to pass, when the LORD has done for my lord according to all the good that He has spoken concerning you, and has appointed you ruler over Israel, that this will be no grief to you, nor offense of heart to my lord, either that you have shed blood without cause, or that my lord has avenged himself" (vv. 30-31).

Abigail was a wise friend. She reminded David that he was destined for Israel's throne.

Scene Three—You Shall Do Great Things and Prevail

When David *endured* and *submitted* to Abigail's rebuke (1 Sam. 25:32-35), his responsive heart was restored. Fortunately for both Saul and David, His faith and faithfulness flourished. David soon faced another trial from King Saul.

Saul received fresh intelligence about David's latest hideout. "*Now the Ziphites came to Saul at Gibeah, saying, 'Is David not hiding in the hill of Hachilah, opposite Jeshimon?'*" (1 Sam. 26:1). In spite of his repentant words and tears a few weeks earlier (1 Sam. 24:16-21), Saul's hypocritical and rebellious heart was revealed. He immediately launched another massive manhunt. "*Then Saul arose and went down to the Wilderness of Ziph, having three thousand chosen men of Israel with him, to seek David in the Wilderness of Ziph*" (1 Sam. 26:2).

Since God's promises were fresh in David's mind, he was not afraid of Saul or his army. He understood that his daily trials with Saul

---

[96]See Chapter 4, "The Father's Look."
[97]See Chapter 6, "The Father's Rebuke: Needed."

were part of his child training. "The LORD," his "shepherd," was preparing him for greater things, and he knew it.

Once again, David's wilderness experience served him well. He and his men were not taken by surprise. They watched Saul's camp, knew when they ate and when they slept. They knew where Saul was sleeping among his troops, and they saw the last watchman doze off.

As Saul and his elite soldiers slept, David boldly walked into Saul's camp, stood by Saul's bed, and took his spear and jug of water from beside his head. David spared Saul's life a second time, in spite of Abishai's protest. Notice how the scene unfolded. David said:

> *"Who will go down with me to Saul in the camp?"*
> *And Abishai said, "I will go down with you."*
> *[7]So David and Abishai came to the people by night; and there Saul lay sleeping within the camp, with his spear stuck in the ground by his head. And Abner and the people lay all around him. [8]Then Abishai said to David, "God has delivered your enemy into your hand this day. Now therefore, please, let me strike him at once with the spear, right to the earth; and I will not **have to strike** him a second time!"*
> *[9]But David said to Abishai, "Do not destroy him; for who can stretch out his hand against the LORD's anointed, and be guiltless?" [10]David said furthermore, **"As the LORD lives, the LORD shall strike him, or his day shall come to die, or he shall go out to battle and perish. [11]The LORD forbid that I should stretch out my hand against the LORD's anointed.** But please, take now the spear and the jug of water that are by his head, and let us go." [12]So David took the spear and the jug of water **by** Saul's head, and they got away; and no man saw or knew **it** or awoke. For they **were** all asleep, because a deep sleep from the LORD had fallen on them* (1 Sam. 26:6-12, emphasis mine).

"We are watching not merely David's daring but Yahweh's hand at work. Saul is helpless because Yahweh made him that way."[98] David proved he was not seeking to kill Saul. He left Saul in God's hands. David's words were full of faith. In fact, they were prophetic (vv. 10-11). God's appointed day for Saul to die in battle was only months away (1 Sam. 31).

David stood at a safe distance from the camp and called out to Saul and his bodyguards. Saul realized that God had delivered him into

---

[98]Davis, *1 Samuel*, 272.

David's hand once again. He also realized that David had spared his life a second time. Saul was alive because of David's mercy, so he called out to David.

> *[21]Then Saul said, "I have sinned. Return, my son David. For I will harm you no more, because my life was precious in your eyes this day. Indeed I have played the fool and erred exceedingly."*
> *[22]And David answered and said, "Here is the king's spear. Let one of the young men come over and get it. [23]May the LORD repay every man for his righteousness and his faithfulness; for the LORD delivered you into my hand today, but I would not stretch out my hand against the LORD's anointed. [24]And indeed, as your life was valued much this day in my eyes, so let my life be valued much in the eyes of the LORD, and let Him deliver me out of all tribulation."*
> *[25]Then Saul said to David, "May you be blessed, my son David! You shall both do great things and also still prevail."*
> *So David went on his way, and Saul returned to his place"* (1 Sam. 26:21-25, emphasis mine).

Wisely, David's faith was not in Saul's fickle promises. His faith was in his Lord. It did not matter whether Saul valued David's life as long as his life was "valued much in the eyes of the Lord" (v. 24).

The responsive heart receives God's promises, no matter who confirms them. Saul confirmed, *"You shall both do great things and also still prevail"* (v. 25).

Conclusion

At every major turn in David's life, he received confirmation of God future plans for him. Why the repeated reminders? God was *training* David to remember the purpose and value of His chastening. He did not want David to *forget, despise,* or *be discouraged* by chastening. He wanted trust and obedience to become David's default response in every difficult situation. He wanted David to think, "This difficulty is the Father preparing and equipping me to fulfill His purpose for my life." He wanted David to be *trained, submit to,* and *endure* His chastening because he respected the Father. He wants the same for you and me.

Chapter 19

STRENGTHEN YOURSELF
IN THE LORD

David did not always respond positively to chastening. But why? Why, for example, was David distracted from the Father's eye when dealing with Nabal (1 Sam. 25), yet he had been sensitive to His eye a short time earlier (1 Sam. 24)? Why then did he run away (1 Sam. 27) from where God had protected him and repeatedly confirmed His purpose for him?

The question is easy to answer if we make it personal. How can you and I yield to a sin after being on a spiritual mountaintop? Anyone who has walked with God, for longer than a few weeks, knows it can happen.

A sobering detail introduced the events in 1 Samuel 25. *"Then Samuel died; and the Israelites gathered together and lamented for him, and buried him at his home in Ramah. And David arose and went down to the Wilderness of Paran"* (v. 1).

Grieving

Could Samuel's death have influenced David's fleshly response to Nabal and his fleeing to Gath? Could Samuel's death have been a link to David's discouragement? Is it normal to have an emotional response to a trusted spiritual mentor's death? I believe it is.

The prophet Samuel anointed David to replace Saul. Perhaps David wondered, "Now that Samuel is dead and Saul is still king and seeking my life, is God's promise still valid?" I believe that would have been my question.

Some of my lowest times have come after the death of someone I counted on for spiritual support. When my mother died, I knew my chief prayer warrior was gone. As long as she was alive, no matter what happened in my ministry, no matter how my faith was tried, I knew Mother was praying for Connie and me and our children. I knew I could call on her and she would have an intimate conversation with the Father. But when she died, I wondered what I would do without her intercession. Maybe David had the same kind of questions.

David may have become insensitive to the Father's eye because Samuel's death left him feeling vulnerable, angry, and abandoned. As a result, when Nabal insulted him, he lashed out in anger. He reacted in the flesh instead of exhibiting spiritual fruit and faithfulness. The Father's rebuke through Abigail refocused David's eyes on the Father's eyes (1 Sam. 25), but the victory was short lived. Soon the Ziphites reported his hiding place to Saul (26:1). Saul launched another massive manhunt, and David mercifully spared Saul's life (26:9-12).

David was filled with faith after observing Saul's miraculous slumber. He was repeatedly reminded of his destiny. Yet, soon he became physically, spiritually, and emotionally exhausted. After Samuel's death, multiple betrayals [the Ziphites betrayed him at least two times], Saul's unrelenting pursuit, and the growing responsibility of caring for 600 men and their families, finally overwhelmed David. He succumbed to fear and sank into despair.

We are the most vulnerable to temptation when emotions control our wills rather than our wills controlling our emotions. We all grieve over the loss of a loved one; it is natural. Be aware that it is a vulnerable time. We can continue to walk by faith and not by our feelings, but only if we maintain a responsive heart.

David's Dilemma

Our focus now returns to David's Dilemma. The Philistines prepared to go into battle against Israel. Several Philistine kings (warlords) combined their armies to fight against Saul. Before the battle, the Philistine kings reviewed the troops. David and his men were with Achish's troops.

150

The princes of the Philistines were angry with him [Achish]*; so the princes of the Philistines said to him, "Make this fellow return, that he may go back to the place which you have appointed for him, and do not let him go down with us to battle, lest in the battle he become our adversary. For with what could he reconcile himself to his master, if not with the heads of these men? Is this not David, of*

whom they sang to one another in dances, saying:
    'Saul has slain his thousands,
        And David his ten thousands'?" (1 Sam. 29:4-5).

The Philistine commanders repeated the song sung in Israel to celebrate David's multiple victories over Philistine forces, including his victory over Goliath of Gath. The Philistine leaders confirmed what David already knew. He had no business being among the Philistine troops. He was their enemy, not their ally. The Father's rebuke was intended to rescue David from himself. He used pagans to deliver the rebuke to His son.

"So David and his men rose early to depart in the morning, to return to the land of the Philistines. And the Philistines went up to Jezreel" (1 Sam. 29:11). David and his men must have felt a great relief leaving the battlefield, headed for home. God had protected them from going into battle against their fellow Israelis. Things seemed to be going well, yet David was turning a blind eye and deaf ear to the Father's chastening. He did not ask God what to do. It appeared he was going back to business as usual. Consequently, the Father used His rod.

The Father's rod came in a shocking form. When David and his men arrived at Ziklag, they found their city in ashes. They searched, found no charred bodies, and realized raiders had kidnapped all of their wives and children (1 Sam. 30:3). They would soon be sold as slaves. *"Then David and the people who **were** with him lifted up their voices and wept, until they had no more power to weep"* (v. 4, emphasis mine).

Restored Fellowship

The Father had David's attention at last. David turned to God, apparently for the first time in sixteen months. When he did, God cleansed him, forgave him, and restored the broken relationship between them.

Even though some of his men blamed him and wanted to stone him, "*David strengthened himself in the LORD his God*" (v. 6). This is a revealing statement, not only for David, but for us as well.

Have a Personal Relationship

How can we strengthen ourselves in the Lord? First, we must have a personal relationship with God.

David received strength from "*the LORD **his** God*" (v. 6). He had a personal relationship with God. He could say, "*The LORD is my shepherd,*" (Ps. 23:1). Can you?

David's personal relationship with God was a faith relationship. He said, "*But the salvation of the righteous is from the LORD; **He is** their strength in the time of trouble. And the LORD shall help them and deliver them; He shall deliver them from the wicked, and save them, because they trust in Him*" (Ps. 37:39-40, emphasis mine). David's reliance on God and his relationship with God were based on his personal trust in God.

Today, we have a personal relationship with God when we place our faith in Jesus Christ. The Bible promises, "*But as many as received Him, to them He gave the right to become children of God, to those who believe in His name*" (John 1:12). Have you trusted Jesus Christ as your Savior? If so, you have a personal relationship with God. You can strengthen yourself in the Lord.

Remember His Promises

How does one strengthen himself or herself in the Lord? Second, we remind ourselves of God's promises. This seems to be what David did. Here we compare Scripture with Scripture.

David was hiding with his six hundred men in the Ziph wilderness, and Jonathan found him. Notice the reason Jonathan sought him out. "*Then Jonathan, Saul's son, arose and went to David in the woods and **strengthened his hand in God**. [How did Jonathan strengthen David in God?] And he said to him, 'Do not fear, for the hand of Saul my father shall not find you. You shall be king over Israel, and I shall be next to you. Even my father Saul knows that'*" (1 Sam. 23:16-17, emphasis mine). Jonathan reminded David of God's promise and plan for his life.

When *"David strengthened himself in the LORD his God,"* obviously he reminded himself of God's plan for his life. He had a personal conversation with himself based on God's revelation.[99]

You and I can strengthen ourselves in the Lord. If we have a personal relationship with God through faith in Jesus Christ, we can remind ourselves of God's promises in His Word. Our Lord Jesus said, *"For assuredly, I say to you, till heaven and earth pass away, one jot or one tittle will by no means pass from the law till all is fulfilled"* (Matt. 15:18). God is 100% faithful to His Word. Claim every promise that applies to you. When you doubt, remind yourself of those promises. Strengthen yourself in the Lord.

Ask God for Direction

Third, ask God what you should do. David finally did what he should have done instead of fleeing to Gath. David called for Abiathar the priest. *"Then David said to Abiathar the priest, Ahimelech's son, 'Please bring the ephod here to me.' And Abiathar brought the ephod to David. So David inquired of the LORD, saying, 'Shall I pursue this troop? Shall I overtake them?' And He answered him, 'Pursue, for you shall surely overtake* **them** *and without fail recover* **all**'" (1 Sam. 30:8, emphasis mine).

David and his men did what God said to do. They pursued the raiders, found them, defeated them, and rescued every one of their families. Not one person was lost (vv. 18-19). They also retrieved all of their stolen property, plus a vast amount of property the raiders had stolen from others.

We too can receive God's directions, encouragement, and comfort. We do not have a priest with an ephod, but we do have a High Priest. The New Testament declares:

> [14]*Seeing then that we have a great High Priest who has passed through the heavens, Jesus the Son of God, let us hold fast* **our** *confession.* [15]*For we do not have a High Priest who cannot sympathize with our weaknesses, but was in all* **points** *tempted as* **we are, yet** *without sin.* [16]*Let us therefore come boldly to the throne of grace, that we may obtain mercy and find grace to help in time of need* (Heb. 4:14-16, emphasis mine).

We can go to our High Priest in times of need. Had David sought the Lord's counsel in his day of discouragement, he would have remained

---

[99]Davis, *1 Samuel*, 313-14.

in Israel among his people. God would have continued to deliver him from Saul daily.

It is easy to see why God said, *"Do not be discouraged when you are rebuked by Him"* (Heb. 12:5). When David became discouraged, he did not endure. He did not stay under the load of God's daily designed trials. He stepped out of God's will.

We are both warned and warmed by the painful season in David's life. David drifted away, but he was restored in a day.

Have you begun to drift spiritually? Return. Confess your sin. Strengthen yourself in the Lord.

Daily Chastening, Daily Dependence

God's goal for us is daily dependence on Him. The months that David lived in the wilderness, hiding from Saul and his soldiers, were invaluable training. David learned more about walking by faith and trusting God for his daily needs than at any other period of his life. Daily trails were intended to teach daily trust.

David's season of chastening, prior to going to Ziklag, was not correction for sin. David's time in the wilderness was a "refining place with God." *"And David stayed in strongholds in the wilderness, and remained in the mountains in the Wilderness of Ziph. Saul sought him every day, but God did not deliver him into his hand"* (1 Sam. 23:14). The negative daily pressures on David's life—*"Saul sought him every day"*—had a positive counter balance—God delivered him daily.

The daily need to look to and depend on God matured David's faith. Being the shepherd-leader, caring for 600 loyal men and their families, was a part of the Father's preparation to make David the shepherd-king of the entire nation.

David's trials were not easy, but they were good for him. Likewise, our trials are not easy, but they are good for us. When we endure, our faith grows. If we surrender to discouragement, our faith falters.

In my forty-plus years of pastoral ministry, I have seen more of Christ's servant-soldiers quit because they were discouraged by the daily battles, than for any other reason. Pastors, deacons, teachers, children's workers, youth workers who once ran well, "grew weary in well doing." Further, discouragement also breaks up many homes. Couples give up on their marriage when they could and should endure.

In contrast, God encourages, *"And let us not grow weary while doing good, for in due season we shall reap if we do not lose heart"* (Gal.

6:9). The Greek root word, translated "lose heart" in Galatians 6:9, is translated "discouraged" in Hebrews 12:5. You get the point. God does not want us to lose heart. We can endure rather than be discouraged.

Amazing Grace

David experienced God's amazing grace when he returned to the Lord from his Ziklag wandering. His responsive heart was restored. All the possessions and people he lost were restored, and even more. No wonder David sang, *"He restores my soul"* (Ps. 23:3).[100]

David returned to Israel with gifts for the villages that had helped him when he was hiding from Saul. In just a few days, Saul died in the battle against the Philistines. Saul finally died by his own hand, not by David's hand (1 Sam. 31). David submitted to the Father's child training; all of Judah came and submitted to David as their king (2 Sam. 2:4).

Conclusion

The Father's chastening is tailor-made for each of us. He knows our futures. He knows His plans for us, and how to prepare us for those plans. To get in on those plans, we can respond to His chastening in positive ways. Instead of *forgetting*, *despising*, and being *discouraged* by chastening, we can *endure*, *submit* to, and *be trained* by His chastening.

Our heavenly Father is pleased with responsive hearts. Responsive hearts are sensitive to His eye, obedient to His Word, and fulfill His greater purpose for their lives. You can have a responsive heart. You can please God. Chastening is the process He uses to develop responsive hearts.

Do you have a responsive heart?

---

[100]See Appendix 3, "Chastening and Psalms 23, 32, & 51"

Appendix 1

Devotional Life

The "devotional life" refers to our daily Bible reading and prayer time. We set aside a time each day to devote our full attention to learning from and listening to God. Some call it a quiet time. The name is not important; the daily practice is the important thing.

How does one have a daily devotional? One helpful suggestion is a six-step process.

1. **Have a specific time and place for your quiet time.** Consider your quiet time an appointment with Christ. . . . If possible, that time should be at the beginning of your day. Your entire day will be different if you begin it with Christ.
2. **Be consistent.** . . . A quiet time . . . is the way you "program" yourself to let Christ be Lord of your life that day.
3. **Have a Bible and a pencil handy.** . . . You probably will want to add a small notebook for keeping a spiritual diary and for making notes about what you have learned and experienced. [Of course, you may prefer to make notes on your computer, tablet, or phone.]
4. **Begin your quiet time with prayer.** Open your heart to Christ. Offer Him the right to teach, to discipline, and to direct you as you study and meditate. . . .
5. **Take time to let Christ speak to you.** Bible reading will always be the central part of your quiet time. . . . Allow Christ to speak to you as you meditate upon His words. . . . [Ask yourself questions about the passage. . . . Simply open your heart and trust the Holy Spirit to teach you as you look for answers to:
   • Is there a truth that should influence (1) what I believe, (2) how I feel, or (3) the way I behave?
   • Is there an example to follow or avoid?
   • Is there a command to obey?
   • Is there a promise to claim?[101]]

End your quiet time with a definite commitment for the day. Decide how you can live out what Christ has revealed to you during your

[101]Ralph W. Neighbour, Jr. and Bill Latham, *SURVIVAL KIT: Five Keys to Effective Spiritual Growth* (Nashville: LifeWay Press, 1996), 8-9.

quiet time. This is a practical way to extend your faith into the way you live your life.[102]

---

[102]Ibid., 7-8.

Appendix 2

A Different World

I grew up in a middle class community in Baton Rouge, Louisiana. Many things about my 1960s neighborhood would look and feel strange today.

Living conditions were different. By today's standards, the cars were huge and the houses were small. An average family had three children but only one bathroom. Few could afford air-conditioning and no one had a walk-in closet. We did not have enough clothes to need one. Only upper middle-class families had a color television, but never more than one. Why would anyone want more than one television? There were only three channels, and you could only watch one at a time. Our TV was black and white, but sometimes it was more gray static than picture. Cable and Dish TV were unknown, as were home computers, the internet, cell phones, and microwaves. We avoided items "Made in Japan." Back then, Japanese products were notorious for their poor quality. We had one telephone and it was in the family room. Many days went by without it ringing.

Family life was different. Single-parent families were rare. Divorces were few. The present-day national tragedy of fatherlessness was unknown. Most families honored Sunday as a day for church attendance. Our street was a Sunday morning Christian parade as eight out of ten families made their way to various churches in our city. No doubt, church attendance was a formality for some; they lacked a personal relationship with Jesus Christ. However, the broad-scale church attendance resulted in a Bible-influenced worldview permeating every part of the culture. The Bible was respected in public school as well as in church.

Children enjoyed childhood. My friends and I played ball for hours nearly every day. We only stayed in the house if we were sick or it was pouring rain. There were a few chunky kids, but not many. No one feared or even imagined an epidemic of childhood obesity. We had never heard of a child-abduction. Children safely roamed the neighborhood unsupervised. We played outside until dark, or suppertime—whichever came first. Families usually ate their evening meals at the same time and around a table. All family members were expected to be present. Many families read the Bible and prayed at suppertime.

Parents were in charge at home. The Principal and the teachers ran the school; they were not afraid of the children. We did not argue with adults, and fathers were the ultimate authority. "My daddy said so" ended many arguments. If one got in trouble at school, corporal punishment was not uncommon. The same was true at home.

My dad took Proverbs 13:24 literally: *"He who spares his rod hates his son, but he who loves him disciplines him promptly."* Dad wanted me to know I was loved. He believed in and practiced corporal punishment, though it was not his only or his most often used form of discipline. The same was true of my friends' dads. Most of us received a few spankings at school and at home, but no one thought it was child abuse. We lived in a different world.

You might be shocked if you could look back on a disciplinary scene in my childhood home. You would hear my dad say, "Truman, go to your room. While you're waiting for me, think about what you did." I heard the command several times and I knew what was coming. It was more than a time-out; I was going to get a spanking.

My responses varied.

Sometimes I was sad. I cried before Dad entered my room.

I was always sorry. I was sorry I was going to be spanked.

Sometimes I was mad—usually at my younger sister for ratting me out.

Sometimes I prepared for my future by padding the seat of my jeans with tissues. A posterior shock absorber was a very present help in time of need and an art form requiring careful calculations. There had to be enough tissue to be beneficial, but not enough to be noticed.

Often I was introspective. I thought about what I had done and I promised myself I would be a better boy in the future. It was comforting to think I would never get in trouble or feel the sting of my father's belt again.

If a few minutes passed, I hoped Dad would forget he sent me to my room. He never did.

When Dad came in, he began with "the talk." I hated the talk. He told me what high hopes he had for me. He explained how my behavior disappointed him and why I required correction. Finally, with his belt in hand, he said in a sad voice, "Son, this is going to hurt me more than it hurts you." At the time, I was unconvinced.

Dad's discipline may disturb you now, but it got my attention then. Eventually, it adjusted my behavior and I learned to respect authority. Contrary to what some child psychologists suggest, Dad's discipline did not make me violent, induce alcoholism and drug abuse, nor did it give me multiple personality disorders.[103] The opposite is true. My love for my dad

---

[103]Ryan Jaslow, "Spanking, physical punishment may raise risk for mental health woes in adult years" (accessed 17 February 2014); available from

grew. I began to understand his heart. He never wanted to hurt me; he wanted to change much more than my behavior. He wanted to change my heart. His various forms of discipline were aimed at helping me become the best man I could be.

Likewise, our heavenly Father disciplines His children. He always corrects us in love, with wisdom, and for our good. He is never harsh or cruel. He is *"touched with the feeling of our infirmities"* (Heb. 4:15 KJV); our weakness and suffering hurts Him more than it hurts us.

Just as my dad wanted me to respond positively to him, God wants you and me to have responsive hearts. It is His goal for us. It is why He disciplines us.

Dad and God's Discipline

Through the years, in my pastoral preaching, I illustrated our heavenly Father's discipline with stories about my dad's discipline. By the way, the idea was not original with me. The Bible makes the connection between parental discipline and God's discipline. It says, *"We have had human fathers who corrected us, and we paid them respect. Shall we not much more readily be in subjection to the Father of spirits and live?"* (Heb. 12:9, emphasis mine).

Early in my pastoral ministry, people identified with stories about my dad's discipline. They understood. They made the connection. Their childhood experiences were similar to mine.

In the later years of my pastoral ministry, particularly in the first two decades of the twenty-first century, I noticed a different response. A growing number of people listened with a note of shock and alarm. They thought my dad's discipline was child abuse. They thought he had no right to spank me.

Over the same time period, I sensed a corresponding shift in attitudes toward God. Many no longer respected God's right to discipline. The idea offended them. They thought a disciplining God would be a spiritual child-abuser. God's job, in their minds, was to make them happy, comfortable, and accommodate their desires. They expected God to give them what they wanted when they wanted it. They expected Him to do whatever was necessary to make them feel good. Anything less, in their judgment, was unloving.

A large study of teenagers in the United States, conducted in 2005, confirmed my observations. The majority of more than 3300 teenagers

http://www.cbsnews.com/news/spanking-physical-punishment-may-raise-risk-for-mental-health-woes-in-adult-years/.

surveyed expressed a view of God, which the researcher labeled, "'moralistic therapeutic deism.' Translation: It's a watered-down faith that portrays God as a 'divine therapist' whose chief goal is to boost people's self-esteem."[104]

> The dominant view, even among evangelical teenagers, is that God made everything and established a moral order, but he does not intervene. . . . They see God as not demanding much from them because he is chiefly engaged in solving their problems and making them feel good. Religion is about experiencing happiness, contentedness, and having God solve one's problems and provide stuff like homes, the Internet, iPods, iPads, and iPhones.[105]

By the way, a therapeutic view of God among teenagers should not surprise us. They inherited their view of God from Baby Boomer, Me Generation grandparents, self-fulfillment focused parents, and churches dominated by "Christianized" pop-psychology. What else would we expect teenagers to believe?

Unfortunately, the idealized, accommodating God, as opposed to the child training God, is disappointing. God does not live up to false expectations. He is faithful to Himself; His character is consistent. We can trust Him to be *exactly* who He revealed Himself to be, but *only* who He revealed Himself to be. He does not cater to false expectations.

Which brings me to the challenge of this book: because of changing attitudes toward parental discipline and God's discipline, you may think this a negative book. I admit that it lacks a warm-fuzzy, feel-good theme. I believe, however, anyone who responds to its message will find genuine joy. It will clarify some of the Father's work in your life, and that will comfort you. It will sweep away some false expectations about your heavenly Father.

Several years ago the content of this book turned the light on for me. I believe it will do the same for you. While our culture's view of parental and divine discipline has changed, God's discipline of His children has not changed and will not change. Recognizing His chastening will help you respond positively to God. If you do, you will experience His supernatural favor in your life and you will begin to see God's greater

---

[104]John Blake, "Author: More teens becoming 'fake' Christians" (accessed 17 February 2014); available from http://www.cnn.com/2010/LIVING/08/27/almost.christian/.

[105]David F. Wells, *God in the Whirlwind: How the Holy-love of God Reorients Our World* (Wheaton: Crossway, 2014), 21.

purpose for you. That is good news, even if it is a little uncomfortable at first.

Appendix 3

Chastening and Psalms 23, 32, & 51

Psalms 23, 32, and 51 should be read in light of David's daily chastening by the Lord. David learned to take comfort in the Father's discipline. He said, "*Your rod and Your staff, they comfort me*" (Ps. 23:4). God used Saul and other troubling people and events in his life. The Good Shepherd used them to prepare David for His greater purpose. Understanding God's chastening process enabled David to say, "*You prepare a table before me in the presence of my enemies*" (v. 5).

In his excellent book, *A Shepherd Looks at the 23rd Psalm*, Phillip Keller shared a drastic form of discipline that shepherds use to save a straying lamb's life. If a straying lamb will not follow the shepherd, it is vulnerable to predators. For the wandering lamb's protection, the shepherd will break one of its front legs. He then binds up the leg and carries the lamb on his shoulders as he leads the flock. As the leg heals, the straying lamb bonds with the shepherd. Once healed, the lamb returns to the flock. The bond of love and discipline has won the heart of the lamb. It no longer strays; it stays nearer the shepherd than any other sheep.

David likely had this discipline in mind when he wrote his poetic confessions in Psalms 32 and 51. He was guilty of adultery and murder. He acknowledged his sin and pleaded for God's mercy and cleansing. He also acknowledged God's purpose in His conviction and chastening. David prayed, "*Purge me . . . wash me . . . make me hear joy and gladness* [and here it is] *that the bones You have broken may rejoice*" (Ps. 51:7-8). David was a shepherd and fully aware of the Father's rod and comfort. He understood that the Father's heavy-hand (Ps. 32:4) was also the Shepherd's healing-wound. The Father was placing His straying lamb on His shoulders. He wanted to bond David's heart with His heart. David understood and his responsive heart was restored. He prayed:

⁸Make me hear joy and gladness,
***That** the bones You have broken may rejoice.*
⁹Hide Your face from my sins,
And blot out all my iniquities.
¹⁰Create in me a clean heart, O God,
And renew a steadfast spirit within me (Ps. 51:8-10, emphasis mine).

There was a period in my life when I let discouragement cause me to resign a church that I deeply loved. For the next three years, David's life and chastening greatly encouraged me. I listened and learned. I overcame discouragement by submitting to the Father's chastening. In the process, I strengthened myself in the Lord. After three years, God graciously restored me to the church I had resigned.

I have learned that being responsive to the Father's eye is better than needing the Father's rebuke. Responding to the Father's rebuke is better than being corrected by the Father's rod. Responding to the Father's rod is better than going home to heaven without completing my mission on earth. These are the four progressive levels of the Father's chastening (discipline, correction, instruction/education, child training). I want to stay on a first level relationship with the Father, but is it possible? Yes. I believe it is.

You and I can maintain responsive hearts if we do not forget, despise, and become discouraged by the Father's chastening. Instead, we can be trained by, submit to, and endure His chastening. The supernatural result will be sensitive, responsive hearts that are tuned to the Father's heart.

Bibliography

Allen, D. L. (2010). *Hebrews in the New American Commentary, vol. 35.* Nashville, TN: Broadman & Holman Publishers

Bergen, R. D. (1996). *1 and 2 Samuel in the New American Commentary, vol. 7.* Nashville, TN: Broadman & Holman Publishers

Blake, J. (2014, February 17). *"Author: More teens becoming 'fake' Christians.* Retrieved from http://www.cnn.com/2010/Living/08/27/almost.christian/

Brown, F., Driver, S.R. and Briggs, C.A. (2000) *Enhanced Brown-Driver-Briggs Hebrew and English Lexicon.* Oak Harbor, WA: Logos Research Systems

Butterfield, R. C. (2012). *The Secret Thoughts of an Unlikely Convert: An English Professor's Journey in Christian Faith.* Pittsburgh, PA: Crown & Covenant Publications

Buzzell, S. S. (1985) *"Proverbs" in the Bible Knowledge Commentary: An Exposition of the Scriptures, vol. 1, eds. Walvoord, J. F. and Zuck, R. B.* Wheaton: Victor Books

Danker, F. W. (2000) *A Greek-English Lexicon of the New Testament and other Early Christian Literature, 3rd ed.* Chicago: The University of Chicago Press

Davis, D. R. (2002) *1 Kings: The Wisdom and the Folly.* Geanies House, Great Britian: Christian Focus Publications

Davis, D. R. (1999). *1 Samuel: Looking on the Heart.* Ross-shire, Scotland: Christian Focus Publications

Ellingworth, P. E. (1993). *The Epistle to the Hebrews, in the New International Greek Testament Commentary.* Grand Rapids: Eerdmans

Ellsworth, R. (2006). *Opening Up Psalms.* Leominster, England: Day One Publications

Gouge, W. (1980). *Commentary on Hebrews.* Grand Rapids, Michigan: Kregel Publications, reprint of 1866 ed.

Haan, M.D., M.R. (1959). *Hebrews, Twenty-six Simple Studies in God's Plan for Victorious Living.* Grand Rapids, Michigan: Zondervan Publishing House

Hodges, Z. C. (1985). *"Hebrews" in the Bible Knowledge Commentary: An Exposition of the Scriptures, vol. 2, Walvoord, J. and Zuck, R. B., eds.* Wheaton: Victor Books

Holloman, H. (2005). *Kregel Dictionary of the Bible and Theology.* Grand Rapids: Kregel Publications

Jaslow, R. (2014, February 17). http://www.cbsnews.com/news/spanking-physical-punishment-may-raise-risk-for-mental-health-woes-in-adult-years/

KJV Bible Commentary. 1994 (E. E. Hindson & W. M. Kroll, Ed.) (124). Nashville, Tennessee: Thomas Nelson

Liddell, H. G. (1996) *A Lexicon: Abridged from Liddell and Scott's Greek-English Lexicon.* Oak Harbor, WA: Logos Research Systems, Inc.

MacArthur, J. (1997). *The MacArthur Study Bible, Revised & Updated, NKJV.* Nashville, Tennessee: Thomas Nelson

MacDonald, W. (1995). *Believer's Bible Commentary: Old and New Testaments* (A. Farstad, Ed.) (88). Nashville, Tennessee: Thomas Nelson

Manser, M. H. (2009). *Dictionary of Bible Themes: The Accessible and Comprehensive Tool for Topical Studies.* London: Martin Manser

Meyers, A. C. (1987). *The Eerdmans Bible Dictionary.* Grand Rapids: Eerdmans

Neighbour Jr., R. W. and Latham, B. (1996). *Survival Kit: Five Keys to Effective Spiritual Growth.* Nashville: LifeWay Press

Oswalt, J. N. (1999). *Theological Wordbook of the Old Testament, Harris, R. L., Archer, Jr., G. l. and Waltke, B. K. eds.* Chicago, IL: Moody Press

Peck, M. S. (1978, 2003). *The Road Less Traveled: A New Psychology of Love, Traditional Values and Spiritual Growth.* New York: Touchstone

Peterson, E. H. (1999). *First and Second Samuel in Westminster Bible Companion, Miller, P. D. and Bartlett, D. L. eds.* Louisville, KY: Westminster John Knox Press

Pink, A.W. (2003). *An Exposition of Hebrews.* Grand Rapids, Michigan: Baker Book House

Pink, A.W. (1977). *The Life of David, Two Volumes in One, Vol. 1.* Swengel, Pennsylvania: Reiner Publications

Radmacher, Earl, D. (2007). *NKJV Study Bible, 2nd Ed.* Nashville: Thomas Nelson

Stein, Robert H. (1993). *Luke in the New American Commentary, vol. 24.* Nashville: Broadman & Holman Publishers

Strong, James. (2001). *Enhanced Strong's Lexicon.* Billingham, WA: Logos Bible Software

Tripp, Paul David. (2012). *Dangerous Calling: Confronting The Unique Challenges of Pastoral Ministry.* Wheaton: Crossway

Wells, David F. (2014). *God in the Whirlwind: How the Holy-love of God Reorients Our World.* Wheaton: Crossway

Wiersbe, Warren W. (2003). *The Bible Exposition Commentary: History.* Colorado Springs, CO: Victor

Wiersbe, Warren W. (1993). *The Essential Everyday Bible Commentary.* Nashville: Thomas Nelson Publishers

Wiersbe, W. W. (1993). *Wiersbe's Expository Outlines on the Old Testament* (Ex 4:18-31). Wheaton, Illinois: Victor Books

Wiersbe, W. W. (1991). *With the Word Bible Commentary* (Ex 1:1). Nashville, Tennessee: Thomas Nelson

Zodhiates, S. (2000). *The Complete Word Study Dictionary: New Testament.* Chattanooga, TN: AMG Publishers

Zodhiates, S. (1992). *The Complete Word Study Dictionary: New Testament, 3rd. Ed.* Chattanooga, TN: AMG Publishers

Websites

"Narcissistic Personality Disorder." (2014, May 6). Retrieved from http://www.mayoclinic.org/diseases-conditions/narcissistic-personality-disorder/basics/definition/con-20025568

Changed Life = Changed Lives!

Pastor Truman's books have been a blessing all over the world and we would like to encourage you to make a purchase for you own personal library or for a friend in need. Pastor Truman advertises by word of mouth, so your testimonies of how God had worked in your life through these workbooks is a powerful tool.

Feel free to contact us at the email address below for more information or to place your order today, visit Amazon.com.

Truman Herring
truherr@comcast.net
www.trumanherringministries.com

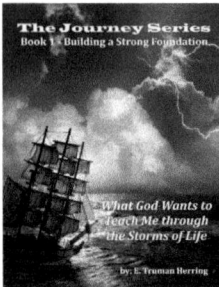

Journey Series – Book 1 – Building a Strong Foundation *– The moment we received the Lord Jesus, we began an amazing journey with God. This journey is with purpose and design to lead us into maturity and fruitfulness. Often overlooked is how God uses the storms of life in the process of growth. This study is design to help us understand six key principles of growing in the storms of life in our journey of walking with Jesus.* ***Cost: $19.99 each plus shipping.***

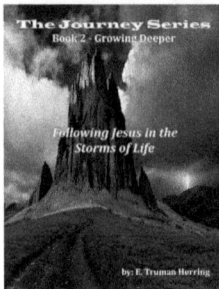

Journey Series – Book 2 – Growing Deeper *– In Book 2 we deal with how Jesus progressively leads his followers to deeper faith and abiding fruitfulness. In the first storm, Jesus would be present in the boat with them. In his section storm, Jesus will send them into the storm alone. Following Jesus means that God is bringing people, places, and events, into our life with purpose. This book will help us better understand and enjoy our Journey with Christ.* ***Cost $19.95 each plus shipping.***

Sound the Alarm

Does God Judge Nations? Will God Judge America?

By: Pastor E. Truman Herring

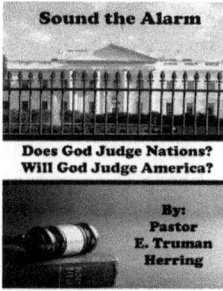

Sound the Alarm – Many Bible believing Christians are grieved and are deeply concerned about the future of America. This book examines the principles of God's judgment of nations and seeks to answer the question: Will God judge America? This book is also a call to hope and prayer that God will revive His Church and heal our nation before it is too late. *Cost: $19.99 each plus shipping*

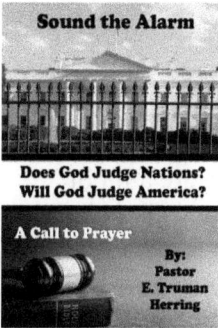

Sound the Alarm

Does God Judge Nations? Will God Judge America?

A Call to Prayer

By: Pastor E. Truman Herring

Sound the Alarm – A Call to Prayer – is a sample edition of 21 of the chapters from Sound the Alarm. To focus on Hope and Intercession for America by including a section at the end of each devotion for you to include your prayers or thoughts of what God is saying to you personally. God is calling many Christians to intercede for America and His Church. Will you be one of them? *Cost: $10.00 each plus shipping*

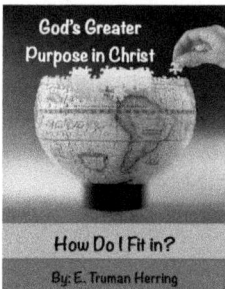

God's Greater Purpose in Christ

How Do I Fit in?

By: E. Truman Herring

God's Greater Purpose in Christ – How Do I Fit In?

Have you found yourself asking, "Do I have a purpose in life? Where do I fit in? Can my life really impact others?"

God's greater purpose is "in Christ," and never apart from Jesus Christ. Any other purpose, no matter how celebrated or successful, is a cheap substitute. By studying the lives of several Bible personalities, whose unique purposes were outlined for them before they were born, we can discover that this same God has a unique purpose for us as well. This book is written to help you discover God's greater purpose for your life! *Cost: $15.00 each plus shipping*

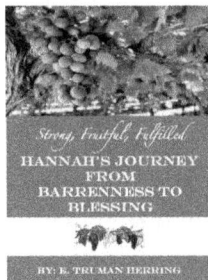

Hannah's Journey from Barrenness to Blessings – ***Strong, Fruitful, Fulfilled*** - What is the secret to being "fruitful?" What does that really mean in your life? Have you desired a more fruitful walk with God? ***Strong, Fruitful, Fulfilled*** magnifies God's great work in the life of Hannah, but it shares the eternal principles that God designed for both men and women. The principles of Scripture drawn from Hannah's struggles and journey of faith will answer your questions. ***Cost: $15.00 each plus shipping***

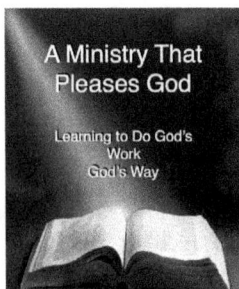

A Ministry That Pleases God – ***Learning to Do God's Work God's Way*** - What's a leader to do when it comes to ministry? There are a lot of suggestions out there for pastors and Christian leaders today. But, how should a leader . . . lead? This is a book for leaders, but more specifically, it is about doing God's ministry God's way. It is written to ministry leaders – not only pastors and church planters, but also for the many other leaders in our churches today. This book reflects a growing conviction that ministry should be done according to God's way in the power of God's Spirit. It is currently in six languages and is given free to church planters in India, Nepal, and some countries in Africa. ***Cost: $15.00 each plus shipping***

www.ingramcontent.com/pod-product-compliance
Lightning Source LLC
Chambersburg PA
CBHW051836090426
42736CB00011B/1826